MW01268890

Women Bishops
of The United Methodist Church

Extraordinary Gifts of the Spirit

Sharon Zimmerman Rader and Margaret Ann Crain

Abingdon Press
Nashville

WOMEN BISHOPS OF THE UNITED METHODIST CHURCH:
EXTRAORDINARY GIFTS OF THE SPIRIT

Scripture quotations unless noted otherwise are taken from the Common English Bible (CEB), copyright 2011. Used by permission. All rights reserved.

Library of Congress Cataloging-in-Publication Data

Info to come

19 20 21 22 23 24 25 26 27 28—10 9 8 7 6 5 4 3 2 1

MANUFACTURED in the UNITED STATES of AMERICA

CONTENTS

PART TWO: WHAT DIFFERENCE DO WOMEN BISHOPS MAKE?

APPENDICES

ACKNOWLEDGMENTS

For Judy,
who encouraged, led, supported, challenged,
and always filled the room with belief, laughter, hope, and joy.
Bishop Judith Craig died just weeks before this book was published.
Her love and presence live on in these pages
to which she gave so much.

*****

A summer lunch near Lake Michigan brought us together for this project. It was a lovely sunny day in a small town in Michigan and we, along with our husbands, were soaking up the sunshine as we chatted. Sharon mentioned her interest in the stories of the first women elected as bishops in a major Christian denomination. Two of the first, Marjorie Matthews and Leontine Kelly, had already died. Others were not getting any younger. "We need to collect these stories," Sharon said, "before they are gone." "Well," said Margaret Ann, "One of my scholarly interests is narrative research, and I love to do interviews. Maybe I could help you!"

And so, it began. Over the course of a year, we began to plan and share our idea with others. We developed a proposal. The General Commission on the Status and Role of Women (GCSRW), headed by General Secretary Dawn Hare, was supportive. Sharon contacted her friends, the earliest bishops still living, and looked for a few days when they might come together to share their stories. GCSRW agreed to support the meeting of the early bishops and United

Methodist Communications agreed to record the conversations and provide transcriptions. The group (our first focus group interview) met in Ohio on April 11-12, 2017. Those two days were rich with story, tears, resolve, and love.

Since then we have interviewed all of the thirty-two living women bishops of The United Methodist Church. They tended to be a bit wary at first but ended up appreciating the opportunity to listen to one another and tell their own stories. Those hours of interviewing and sharing were precious and holy times. We are very grateful to the bishops who gave us their time and their stories. Each one has had an opportunity to see the story of her election as it appears here and to request changes or corrections in the narrative. Appendix A provides a list of the interviews. GCSRW (especially Rev. Leigh Goodrich), the UM General Commission on Archives and History, Wespath and UM Communications have supported and encouraged us all the way. Chris Bethke and Lynn Lubkeman from the Wisconsin Conference, as well as David Lundquist and Barbara Troxell shared important historical documents. Bishop Gregory Palmer and his colleagues in West Ohio provided wonderful hospitality for the first three interviews. Phone interviews with Nancy Grissom Self, Barbara Troxell, Lynn Scott, Stephanie Hixon, Barbara Campbell, and Anita Wood helped us with context and history. Others shared memories via email. And Abingdon Press has graciously agreed to publish this. We are grateful to our editors: Mary Catherine Dean, Barbara Dick, Mickey Frith, and Brittany Sky. We are grateful to our husbands, Blaine and Jack, who have supported the project all the way, including cooking meals for us while we wrote and talked and edited. Most of all, we are grateful to each other. This has been a wonderful journey. Thanks be to God for the opportunity!

Prologue

"THE UNITED METHODIST CHURCH
WILL HAVE BISHOPS WHO ARE WOMEN."

The organization of Methodists in the United States began officially in 1784 with the Christmas Conference held in Baltimore, Maryland. If women attended, their names do not appear in the journal of that conference of American preachers.[1] It would be nearly two hundred years until the first gathering of United Methodist clergywomen was held in January 1975, in Nashville Tennessee.

The 1975 Consultation was envisioned, planned, and staffed by the General Commission on the Status and Role of Women with support from United Methodist Women and the General Board of Higher Education and Ministry and was held at Scarritt College in Nashville, Tennessee. Finding the names, addresses and records of all the United Methodist clergywomen yet living, in order to invite them to the Consultation, became a major and time-consuming task. Staff members of the General Board of Pensions devoted hours and days to combing through paper records of active and retired clergy to find the women who had been ordained beginning in 1889. There was no easy sorting of clergy by gender. The goal was to invite every United Methodist clergywoman to the Consultation.

Just under three hundred persons attended the Consultation, including bishops (all male), denominational staff, ecumenical colleagues, and the press. Excitement and wonder were palpable as the women gathered. None had ever seen or been with so many clergywomen in one place. One woman curtailed her honeymoon to attend. Another left a hospital bed. One woman arrived on crutches. Others brought their babies and young children. Some of the women had been retired (or shut out of) ministry for years while many were in their first five years of serving in The United Methodist Church.

Some women who traveled to Nashville that January were pastors in conferences where they were the first or only woman to serve. Many had never heard another ordained woman preach or lead in worship. Only two women had ever been appointed as district superintendents (regional supervisors of clergy and congregations). Clergywomen serving in United Methodist denominational leadership were almost non-existent.

Workshops on understanding United Methodist structure, women's leadership, biblical interpretation, church history, feminist hymn and liturgy writing, and worship were filled to overflowing at the Consultation. Most women attended whatever event was on the schedule; few chose to "play hooky" by going shopping, sleeping in, or taking a nap. The Consultation provided opportunities to see, be with, and learn from other women in the church and everyone present wanted to take full advantage of the experience.

Late in the week, Dr. Peggy Way, United Church of Christ pastoral theologian, spoke to the group. Beginning her lecture, she stood, looked over the auditorium, and said: "My God! You all look exhausted. Didn't anyone tell you? You don't have to attend everything?" The room erupted in laughter as the women recognized how important the event was to their personal lives as well as to the ministry to which they had been called.

The Consultation was about more than worship, learning and fellowship, however. Attendees were also eager to call the denomination to greater recognition of and support for women's full participation and leadership in The United Methodist Church, particularly that of clergywomen. Concerns were raised, and legislation was developed calling for:

4

- New procedures in support of clergy couples and equitable salaries
- Language in liturgy and worship that included women
- Opportunities for women as lead pastors in larger membership congregations
- Women on the faculties of United Methodist seminaries.

And then, on the last day, someone proposed that United Methodist clergywomen begin to identify and work toward the election of three women from three different regions of the United States to be bishops of the church. The gathered women again laughed. But this time it was nervous laughter.

Women bishops? (By what name would they be called? The word *bishop* is masculine in some languages.) Did women have enough experience to be elected to the office? (Maybe not as much experience in ordained ministry as had been traditionally expected of men, yet some had other, earlier, professional leadership roles.) Would annual conferences accept and be guided by a woman assigned as bishop? (Some conferences were still struggling to appoint a woman to parish ministry in any role other than associate pastor or leader of small rural congregations.) What about a woman's responsibilities as wife, mother, grandmother? (And could a single woman possibly be elected to the episcopacy?) What would a woman bishop wear? (Wait! Male bishops had historically been wearing "dresses"/robes. But earrings and other jewelry? And would the white alb, favored by many women, be appropriate apparel?) There *was* nervous laughter and many questions. But some wondered: "Why not a woman bishop?"

Responding to what some thought of as the "sassiness"[2] emerging from the Consultation, laity and clergy across United Methodism began to seriously consider whether a person's gender should prevent her or him from being set apart for the servant leadership of episcopal oversight and supervision called for in *The Book of Discipline of The United Methodist Church.*

Earlier in 1972, the General Conference had established a Commission to Study Offices of the Episcopacy and District Superintendency. The United Methodist Church had been formed from a merger of the former Evangelical

5

United Brethren and Methodist denominations in 1968, and there was a strong belief that clarity and purpose regarding bishops and superintendents needed to be addressed with "particular reference to the method of their selection, tenure, assignment, function, and such other matters as it shall deem appropriate."[3] The Commission members unanimously agreed that the scope and purpose of the study "should not be limited to the functional and mechanical aspects of the offices of episcopacy and district superintendency but [also]include broad and fundamental issues of episcopacy and district superintendency historically, theologically, biblically, philosophically, and ideally."[4]

The report of the Commission to the 1976 General Conference was an important one and consumed a significant portion of the conversation and debate of that gathering in Portland Oregon. Reflecting on the state of the church and the world, the Commission admitted there was a strong climate that held both "a suspicion of and cry for leadership."[5] The old ways of understanding episcopacy and leadership were changing. Individualistic and autocratic leadership was no longer desired. Women were beginning to enter into superintending roles. And while bishops were responsible for ordering the life of the whole church as well as general supervision, that supervision was always to be *shared* work with peers" [emphasis author's].[6]

Offering a changing understanding of the characteristics of bishops, the Commission used phrases such as: companions, enablers, and exemplars; persons who articulate issues clearly and read consensus competently; negotiates settlements honestly; consults willingly; makes difficult decisions candidly; offers spiritual leadership providing models of living to cope with this age . . . and forging new ways to incarnate the lordship of Jesus Christ. Such descriptors allowed women to begin to be able to envision themselves in episcopal leadership.

With the dreams of the 1975 Clergywomen's Consultation and the decisions of the May 1976 General Conference in mind, the jurisdictional (regional) conferences which have responsibility for electing bishops in the United States convened for their quadrennial conferences in the summer of 1976. At least two women did receive votes for election as bishop that year and other women were beginning to hear "whispers" that they should consider making themselves available at some future time. No woman was elected in 1976, but the possibility was beginning to take shape. Nothing in church law prevented women who had been ordained as elders in full connection from being elected to the tasks of a bishop. Bishops were to equip the church, order the church's life, and enable the gathered church to worship and evangelize.

The Rev. Jeanne Audrey Powers (1932–2017), from the North Central Jurisdiction of The UMC had received significant votes for election to the episcopacy in both the 1972 and 1976 jurisdictional conferences, but it was an "honor she declined."[7] Summarizing her life in the worship bulletin for the memorial service held for her in Mankato, Minnesota on November 11, 2017, Dr. Bruce Robbins wrote:

> In 1958, she was ordained in Minnesota as a deacon in the Methodist Church. When ordained an elder in 1961, she was among the very first women in the Methodist church granted full clergy rights. She was the state director of the Minnesota Methodist Student Movement as well as the Wesley Foundation Campus Minister of the U of Minnesota, creating gathering spaces where students lived and worked together as she challenged them to risk unfamiliar territory and broaden their horizons. She staffed the Methodist Board of Missions where she gave leadership to an ongoing exciting way for young adults to serve in missions for a shorter formative period of their lives . . . was a key representative to the World Council of Churches, was a guiding force in the creation of "Baptism, Eucharist and Ministry," a document that has prompted reform and convergence among Catholic, Orthodox, and Protestant Christians since its approval in 1982 . . . was vice president of the National Council of Churches chairing its Faith and Order Commission for six years . . . she was a member of the UM Commission on the Status and Role of Women, organized in 1973. She was committed to feminist issues. Until her death she was a driving force in the Reconciling Ministries Movement, and she came out as a lesbian during her sermon at its national gathering in 1995. . . . she worked tirelessly for election of the first openly gay UMC bishop, Bishop Karen Oliveto. "Jeanne Audrey was a fierce she-roe who paved the way for so many of us in the church," said Bishop Oliveto. "She taught me to make room for others, always, as well as the importance

7

of mentoring. I loved laughing and debating with her. It was all done with great love and passion and I always learned so much." . . . (When accepting Boston University School of Theology's honor as a "Pioneer Woman" and Anna Howard Shaw Award), [Powers] said "I have chosen to swim against the stream in many areas of controversy because I truly believe that the Church is the Body of Christ, called to share its message of healing, reconciliation, and yes, salvation . . . I do not choose the Church simply because I want to belong, but because I believe in its transforming Spirit."   *(Jeanne Audrey)*

In the 1970s, Powers did not believe the church was yet ready to be open to affirming her full personhood, did not want to be hurtful to the church or her partner, and yes, loved the church so deeply that she did not want to cause the disruption that would occur if she made plain her sexual givenness. "It's not my calling, not my journey in life to do this," she told those who believed she had the gifts and clear evidence of God's grace to be a bishop. She knew she could not be fully herself, living openly and freely in the office of bishop. Powers did, however, mentor many others, including Sharon Rader, reminding them of their privilege and responsibility. "You will have opportunities to sit in rooms where others of us cannot," she told Rader. "Your responsibility is to share the voices and perspectives of those of us who are not there."

In 1976, following the reading of election results that indicated she was the fourth highest vote getter on the first ballot with ninety-one votes, Powers (with the hopes of the resolutions from the Clergywomen's Consultation echoing in her mind) stood to read her Withdrawal Statement to the North Central Jurisdiction Conference:

✳ The United Methodist Church *will* have bishops who are women.
This is not an easy statement to make, nor has the struggle to come to such a decision been made without anguish. I love the Church, and I want to be in its ministry. I cannot conceive of *not* being so. But in assessing my own vocational calling and personal goals, the episcopacy becomes a painful problem.

The struggle in facing up to this possibility is extremely important on behalf of all women. There are numerous women who carry enormous professional responsibility within the Church—some with national visibility and thus electability—but many of them are *lay* women. And there are many ordained women, highly competent in fulfilling their calling (some of them are on the floor of this conference), but because they have not yet had the visibility, you do not know their names nor the gracefulness of the special gifts they bring to their ministry.

In the not too distant future, these qualities are going to coalesce in individual women: ordination, experience, competency, and visibility. But one thing still will be a necessary requirement: the desire, the intentionality, the clear conviction under the guidance of the Holy Spirit that "Yes, I want to serve as a bishop."

As for me, I do not want to do so. My vocation in the ministry is single-minded, but it has taken many forms. I do not want to limit my ministry to one form of expression the rest of my life.

But more than that, I've come to realize that however one expresses her (or his) calling to the ministry, there must lie within it a sense of fulfillment and joy, of being a whole and healthy person at one's deepest center, if that ministry is to be effective. To guard the place of silence and inner collectedness so that the continuous prodding of the Holy Spirit might be heard AND ALSO to live freely and freshly in *our* time is no easy task for anyone. To do so as a bishop must be infinitely harder. To do so as a woman bishop would require of me the toll of a quality I prize the most: a sense of well-being. Without it I do not think I could be the kind of bishop our church needs.

The United Methodist Church *will* have bishops who are women. It will because it needs them. The Council of Bishops will embody inclusiveness, wholeness, and collegiality as both reality and symbol of that community of women and men we know as the Body of Christ.

And when that time comes, when not just one token woman, but *many* women join their brothers in the episcopal procession, we will know that the brokenness we experience now will have been laid before God for healing and growth for us all.[8]

Many in the 1970s were sad that Powers would not allow herself to be a candidate, but those who knew her best understood why. And then, in 1995, when she preached for a Reconciling Ministries gathering and shared with all her identity as a lesbian, everyone understood. Jeanne Audrey Powers had the experience, the skills, and the clear evidence of God's transforming love that would have made her an excellent bishop, but the church was not yet ready for the fullness of who she was, and Powers knew that.

Another woman who was encouraged to make herself available for election was Rev. Barbara Troxell. An early woman leader in her annual conference in the western United States (California-Nevada), by the early 1980s, she was a district superintendent, and a well-known speaker and workshop facilitator. Still, like Powers, Troxell found that as she began to claim her authority as a clergywoman, she had to choose between outer claims and inner witness.

Many colleagues felt she would be an excellent bishop, a pioneer in church leadership. There were others who were not so sure. For some, hesitation stemmed from what they believed was an error on the part of Bishop Marvin Stuart in appointing her as a district superintendent in 1978, especially since she had not served a United Methodist congregation within the bounds of the California-Nevada Conference. Other colleagues felt that her appointment to serve as a district superintendent was excellent and needed; it was "about time there was a woman on the cabinet," they said. Still, Troxell remembers there were also clergy colleagues in California-Nevada who felt her appointment to the superintendency was "a really bad move."

Between 1978 and 1984, Troxell was exploring deeply the possibility of making herself available for election to the episcopacy. Others affirmed, and she came to know, she could do the work of a bishop. Troxell had wide ministry experience to bring to the office of bishop. Her first appointment had been to Cold Spring Harbor Methodist Church in the New York Conference, and then she was appointed to campus ministry at Ohio Wesleyan. She moved to California and transferred to the California-Nevada Conference in 1971, when she became campus minister at Stanford University. (Those were the days when UM congregations were still testing the waters on whether women should even be ordained.) But the inner witness, made known through prayer and consultation with friends whose wisdom she trusted, consistently led her to say no. Becoming bishop was not the calling for her. Her soul needed tending, which she did not believe could be achieved in the episcopacy. "This just did not feel right," and she worried she might lose her soul if elected a bishop. Further, she claimed her desire to find a life-partner and could not envision how that would be possible if she were a bishop! "The request and urging by others for me to let myself be available for possible election as bishop kept happening" into the early 1990s. "Each quadrennium when it was raised, I found myself discerning and pondering again. Each time the inner witness came up as *no*."

There were others, including Rev. Lynn Joselyn (Maine Annual Conference, Northeast Jurisdiction), and Rev. Dr. Diedra Kriewald (Virginia Annual Conference, Southeast Jurisdiction), who were also committed to the belief that the church would be more whole, more faithful if women were affirmed for leadership at the church's highest levels. They allowed themselves to be part of the discernment processes in their respective jurisdictions, becoming signs to the church of the possibility of additional women in the Council of Bishops. But the church was only beginning to allow itself to contemplate the possibility of women's leadership in the episcopacy, and they were not elected.

What follows in part 1 of this book are the stories of how thirty-four women have been elected bishop in The United Methodist Church. We have chosen to focus on the election stories because some of the earliest ones are in danger of being lost. These stories reveal a great deal about our church and its processes. Each bishop has reviewed her story as presented here. A song, "Ones Who've Gone Before Us," which was sung in those gatherings of clergywomen, captures the importance of telling these stories:

> There are times we reach the edge of a turning point, a breaking through,
> There are times we cannot see what's just ahead, but still we know,
> We have a course that's clear, a path to follow, and we must go
> (and we must go . . .)

CHORUS:
And the ONES WHO'VE GONE BEFORE US will show us the way,
The ones who follow after will welcome the new day.
And the ONES WHO'VE GONE BEFORE US will join in the chorus,
When we do, when we make it through.

There are times the burden's heavier than we can bear, but we hold on,
Because we know there is a task at hand which must be done.
There are times our problems build up and start to shake us, threaten to
 break us,
'Til we remember it's only dancin' through that will remake us
 (that will remake us ...)

CHORUS
There are times it's almost easier to despair, to close our eyes
But when we look around and see we're not alone, our spirits rise.
There are times we get so tired of waiting any longer,
But we know we're building as we grow, we're getting stronger
 (we're getting stronger ...)

CHORUS
(repeat Chorus)[9]

The analysis chapters in part 2 of this book rely on the complete interview data that we collected from all the living bishops. They engaged in conversations that ranged widely and were often intense with deep sharing. We sensed that we were on holy ground. At times, someone would ask us to turn off the tape recorder so that what she needed to say would not be on the record. Yet, *we* heard all that, and it has helped us to see what has happened in the church and what might be important issues for the future. We have honored the confidentiality of those moments but expect that the insights have made their way into this book somehow. The interviews will be available for further study when they are deposited with the Commission on Archives and History, after the completion of this book.

Ones who've gone before us will show us the way, and ones who follow after will welcome the new day.

Notes

1. John Atkinson, *Centennial History of American Methodism* (New York: Phillips & Hunt, 1884), 34–50. http://tiny.cc/prob2y, accessed January 9, 2019.

2. Interview with Nancy Grissom Self, July 10, 2018. Self was part of the General Secretariat of the General Commission on the Status and Role of Women and described the gathering by saying, "Weren't we sassy?"

3. *The Daily Christian Advocate* 1976, Advance Edition, book F, "Bishops and District Superintendents Study Commission 1972-1976," 7.

4. *ADCA* 1976, 7.

5. *ADCA* 1976, 7.

6. *ADCA* 1976, 13.

7. Worship bulletin, Jeanne Audrey Powers, Mankato Minnesota, November 11, 2017.

8. The Rev. Jeanne Audrey Powers, from a speech at the 1976 North Central Jurisdictional Conference, July 15, 1976. A copy of the Withdrawal Statement was obtained from the Wisconsin Conference Archives and History Office.

9. "Ones Who've Gone Before Us," words and music by Doris J. Ellzey (Blesoff), © 1975 Doris Ellzey (Blesoff). Used by permission.

Part One

STORIES OF THE ELECTION
OF WOMEN BISHOPS

1980

MARJORIE SWANK MATTHEWS

The North Central Jurisdiction was first to elect a woman as a bishop. Clergywomen and many others, both lay and clergy, both women and men, had advocated for this for years. Sharon Rader was there and experienced this exciting moment. Other candidates, both men and women, stepped aside to allow Marjorie Swank Matthews to be elected to the episcopacy. Word spread that The United Methodist Church had broken this barrier as it made the national news.

Marjorie Swank Matthews

Four hundred sixty delegates, one-half lay and one-half clergy, representing fourteen annual conferences in the U.S. Midwest gathered in July 1980 at the Convention Center in Dayton, Ohio. The delegates, twenty-three of whom were clergywomen, came from North and South Dakota, Minnesota, Iowa, Illinois, Indiana, Wisconsin, Michigan, and Ohio. The election of three clergy to be bishops of The United Methodist Church was the major item of business for the gathering. Balloting had begun on Tuesday, July 15. Thirteen candidates, including one woman, initially made themselves available for consideration, but three had withdrawn by the time the conference adjourned after four ballots that evening. No one had been elected.

Immediately after worship on Wednesday, July 16, voting began again. Another nine ballots were taken until Rev. Edwin C. Boulton was elected to the episcopacy on the thirteenth ballot. A celebration took place, and then the voting resumed. Two more bishops needed to be elected. Wednesday passed and Thursday began.

Three candidates of those originally in consideration had withdrawn, and three new candidates, one of them a second woman, entered the process and quickly withdrew. The election process involved prayer before each ballot, interviews with nominees, caucusing and negotiating among annual conference delegations. The election of the remaining two bishops became hotly contested. According to *The Christian Advocate*:

> A deadlock developed, with substantial numbers of votes going to six nominees. Dr. Emerson Colaw from the West Ohio Conference and Dr. Marjorie Matthews from the West Michigan Conference were the two front runners.
>
> Finally, after the 24th ballot produced no changes, and with the [scheduled] consecration service just three hours away, Dr. Leigh Roberts, Madison WI, chairperson of the Committee on Episcopacy, announced that the six leaders in vote-getting had just met with conference delegation representatives.
>
> He said all shared "concern for our process and our failure to move ahead. It is suggested that we cease any further caucusing, that this particular practice stop within our delegations, and from this point forward we not vote as groups, in a collective manner, not as delegations, but as individuals, and that each person, with the information they have, continue to vote as the Holy Spirit guides."
>
> The 28th ballot brought a commanding lead (for both Dr. Colaw and Dr. Matthews). The 29th ballot—which tied the record established by the South Central Jurisdiction in 1948 for number of ballots cast for any episcopal election—found Dr. Colaw eight votes away from election and Dr. Matthews 26 votes out.

Four additional candidates were still receiving significant numbers of votes. Each in turn withdrew after the 29th ballot. Dr. Rueben P. Job [one of the final four] moved that the two top candidates be elected by acclamation.

Thunderous applause followed his motion. However, Bishop Ralph Alton who was presiding said such a motion was not in order. Thereupon, Lester C. Mealiff, Des Moines, Iowa, of the Committee on Elections moved the conference rules be suspended and the elections be by acclamation.

Again, applause broke out and at 6:09 pm EDT on July 17, 1980 Bishop Alton declared Bishops Colaw and Matthews to have been elected by acclamation. [It was the greatest number of ballots that had ever been taken for an episcopal election.][1]

Sharon Zimmerman Rader, who had been ordained in 1978, was a reserve clergy delegate from the West Michigan Conference to the jurisdictional conference and had spent most of the conference sitting in the bleachers of the auditorium, watching with anxiety and hope for the future of her church.

At Matthews' election she could be seen weeping and laughing and jumping (dangerously) up and down from her seat in the balcony. Dr. Marjorie Matthews, a clergy member of the conference to which Sharon belonged, had just been elected the *first* woman bishop in The United Methodist Church, the *first* woman in Anglican or Protestant traditions, and perhaps the "first in Christendom since at least the twelfth century," according to NEWSCOPE, the weekly United Methodist newspaper.[2] Looking down on the conference floor, where Bishop Matthews had been sitting with the West Michigan delegation, Rader noticed Matthews' seat was empty. She was being escorted from her place as a delegate up to the platform where she would be greeted by her bishop colleagues as a new member of the Council of Bishops.

The leader of the West Michigan delegation caught Rader's tear-filled eyes and motioned to her to leave her place in the balcony and join the delegation on the floor of the conference. He invited Rader, a reserve delegate, to move to the chair that had just been vacated by the newly elected bishop, Marjorie Swank Matthews. Rader joined the delegation, and together they continued to laugh and cry and rejoice in the election of their friend and colleague. One delegate hugged Rader and whispered, "Enjoy this moment and remember, Sharon, because someday . . ."

Following the greeting and welcoming of the two new bishops from the North Central Jurisdiction into the Council of Bishops, the conference itself was concluded in order to prepare for the evening's service of consecration for the three newly elected bishops.

Quickly, Bishops Colaw and Matthews were directed to another room where they could be interviewed by both church and secular press. Time was passing rapidly, and the consecration service for the three new bishops was to begin at 7:30 pm! There would be no opportunity for a leisurely supper, or for a return to the hotel for a change of clothes and preparation for the consecration service. Bishop Matthews asked Rader and another West Michigan woman clergy colleague to help her through the tumultuous hour before the consecration service was to begin. While one woman went to find Matthews something to eat, Rader was given Matthews' room key at the hotel and instructed to collect a fresh dress and Matthews' clergy robe, neglecting to ask for her "dress up" shoes. Thus, Matthews was consecrated in the comfortable "ropey" sandals she had worn throughout the past three days of conference.

Reporting on Bishop Matthews' election, *The Christian Advocate* had this to say:

> The woman believed to be the first ever elected bishop of a major Christian church in the U.S. [later determined to be world] described her election as a "gigantic step for womankind" and a leap in the church's "understanding of theology."
>
> Bishop Marjorie S. Matthews told reporters at a news conference following her election July 17 that she was "personally proud and made humble by this sacred honor. This is a very historic event," Bishop Matthews said. "It has been 100 years since the first woman was ordained in our church (referring to the 1880 ordination of Anna Howard Shaw in the former Methodist Episcopal Church). Women were not allowed to be full ministerial members of annual conferences until 1956. This election is

a recognition that equality is coming to women in The United Methodist Church."

Bishop Matthews predicted she will bring a new "style" to the episcopacy and said that in the absence of "models" for women bishops she will "have to make (her) own way." . . .

Nancy Grissom Self, a member of the general secretariat of the Commission on the Status and Role of Women [of The UMC], said of the election: "God has blessed the church with a bishop who can speak on behalf of those so far silent in the Council of Bishops. God has sent her there to prepare the way for the shared ministry of women and men in the Council of Bishops. It is a tribute to the North Central Jurisdiction."

Bishop Roy C. Nichols, president of the Council of Bishops, said, ". . . The election of Marjorie Matthews is a giant step in the direction of a fully inclusive church at every level. If all who qualify may become members of our church, then all who qualify should have an opportunity to serve as bishops. I believe God is pleased with the election of a woman bishop."[3]

Following seventeen years employment with an auto parts manufacturer, Matthews had attended and received a bachelor's degree from Central Michigan University, a degree from Colgate-Rochester Divinity School, and both a master's degree in Religion and a Ph.D. from Florida State University. She was ordained an elder in The Methodist Church in 1965 at the age of 49 and served congregations in New York, Florida, Georgia and Michigan and was a district superintendent (only the second woman to do so in all of United Methodism) in the West Michigan Conference at the time of her election to the episcopacy. According to *The Flyer*, at her consecration, Bishop Matthews celebrated the 1880 ordination of the first Methodist clergy woman, Anna Howard Shaw, noting the arduous, one-hundred-year journey between the two milestones. Matthews also counted among her notable foremothers Margaret Henrichsen, the first woman Methodist District Superintendent and Jeanne Audrey Powers, who was the first Methodist woman to receive votes in an episcopal ballot.[4] Following her election and consecration, Matthews was assigned to the Wisconsin Area to become its episcopal leader.

According to *The Flyer*, "The venerable *New York Times* put Matthews on page six. She made *Newsweek* magazine and, of course, the United Methodist media. The *National Catholic Reporter* took note of this '64-year-old-grandmother' who had become an episcopal leader. And *Christian Century* magazine ran a two-page editorial about this 'improbable episcopal choice.' "[5]

Bishop Matthews served as an active bishop for four years in the Council of Bishops. While active and because of her unique position, she traveled worldwide, preaching and sharing with church leaders, laypeople, and children her call to ministry and her responsibilities as a bishop. In 1983, she was the first woman bishop to address the World Council of Churches at its Sixth Assembly held in Vancouver, Canada.

Matthews once jokingly reflected on the language of the denomination that described active bishops as in "effective relationship," which (she pondered aloud) might mean retired bishops were in the "ineffective relationship." Matthews retired in 1984, and in her retirement, she continued to participate in the life of the Council of Bishops. She also traveled, taught, lectured, and preached widely for two more years until a recurrence of breast cancer claimed her life on June 30, 1986.

Judy McCartney, laywoman and chairperson of the East Ohio Commission on the Status and Role of Women, attended the funeral service for Matthews on July 3, 1986 and recorded the following reflections:

> I was almost as surprised at finding myself on the way to Alma, Michigan for a memorial service for Bishop Marjorie Matthews as I had been six years earlier to be present at the historic moment when she was elected to the episcopacy. . . . Though committed in a rational way to the Christian feminist view, I had not allowed my emotions to bind me too securely to feminism or to Marjorie Matthews. . . .
>
> In Dayton, 1980, the questions had been, "Is she the right person to be the 'first'? Is this the right time?" On the way to Alma the questions were: "Had it made any difference to have had a woman as Bishop? Why is this Memorial Service in a place so difficult to reach?"

Then the worship, the Word, the testimony—now the response: for me a Yes! Yes! Yes!

Here we gathered—laity, clergy, bishops—in the church where Marjorie Matthews was nurtured, where she married, baptized a son, sang in the choir, served on committees. She was as one of us. At age 42 she put aside a comfortable, lucrative life as an executive secretary to answer a call to ordained ministry. I wondered how long she had not responded because of the obstacles put before women who did. Early on, many women coming to ministry were older, second-career women. But this day, sitting next to me [was] a young clergy woman, and in that gathering many others, their journey made easier by the "firsts" who had gone before.

Now the tributes and testimony of her kindred friend Ellen [Brubaker] and of clergy who had shared in Marjorie's life let those of us who knew her only dimly see almost face to face the *joie de vivre*, the undaunted stepping out and the discipleship of Bishop Matthews.

All are called, but only a few are chosen to do what Marjorie Matthews did. Called apart for a time for great tasks, she had returned "home" to be in the large company of the least. Bishop Hunt [then President of the Council of Bishops] generously acknowledged that even her colleagues in the Council of Bishops could not comprehend fully the burdens of being the first, or almost the first. Had we supported her enough? Two more women Bishops sat among us that day. Cause for celebration, for prayers for them. Yes!

The words and music of worship washed over me, awakening buried emotion. The words of "Be Thou My Vision," recast to be so generously inclusive—Yes! The clergy stood to sing "All Hail the Power" and for the first time in my memory, enough women's voices were in the blend to be heard. Yes!

Thanks be to God for the firsts of Marjorie Matthews' life! They are a Yes! for all the women who can stand on her small shoulders of broad courage in days to come.[6]

Notes

1. *The Christian Advocate*, North Central Jurisdiction of The United Methodist Church, Second Issue, July 15-17, 1980. "Three Clergy Elected to Episcopacy," 2.

2. As quoted in *The Christian Advocate*, North Central Jurisdiction of The United Methodist Church, issue 2, (Dayton, Ohio, 1980).

3. *The Christian Advocate*, 2.

4. Commission on the Status and Role of Women, *The Flyer* [hereafter, *The Flyer*] 2, no. 4 (August 31, 1980): 1.

5. *The Flyer*: 1, 5.

6. *The Flyer*, 8, no. 3 (August-September 1986): 1, 5.

1984

LEONTINE T. C. KELLY, JUDITH CRAIG

Bishop Matthews' election had opened the door just a small bit. By 1984, across the church, more and more women and some men were increasingly committed and active in lifting up and electing women to the episcopacy. But many men and women continued to resist accepting women into church leadership at all levels.

Leontine T. C. Kelly

Leontine T. C. Kelly was an African American woman in the Virginia Conference who had struggled under the fetters of racism and sexism. A preacher's kid; a pastor's wife, then divorced; a second marriage to another pastor; mother; teacher; denominational executive; and much in demand as a speaker and preacher—Kelly found herself increasingly traveling across the church. Angella Current, describing her mother's (Kelly's) journey into greater and greater responsibility and leadership, says, "Many persons, in and out of the Church, began to recognize and respond to the proclaiming of the gospel through this new and anointed voice that called them to remember and live their covenant relationship with God."[1]

Kelly was encouraged by women in the Southeastern Jurisdiction of the denomination to allow herself to become available for consideration as an episcopal candidate. "Recognizing the risk of ridicule, she allowed her name to be placed in nomination at the 1980 jurisdictional conference. Veteran power brokers for episcopal elections were *shocked* [emphasis author's]; they felt her nomination audacious, as well as ridiculous, and she was not elected."[2]

A third Clergywomen's Consultation was attended by seven hundred fifty women in Glorietta, New Mexico in 1983. Co-chaired by Rev. Kelly and Rev. Sharon Brown Christopher, the Consultation considered and then affirmed a resolution to endorse Rev. Kelly for the episcopacy. Acknowledging the resistance to the election of a woman (and an African American woman at that), which had been generated in the earlier 1980 Southeastern Jurisdictional Conference, women at the Clergywomen's Consultation devised a new strategy. Her name would be placed in nomination in four of the five jurisdictions that would gather in July 1984. Women across the southeast were encouraged to support Kelly, as were Black Methodists for Church Renewal. Again, Current says, "Many of these leaders were ambivalent toward her candidacy because they feared that her being a black woman would negatively affect the candidacy of the black men aspiring for the episcopacy and reduce their chances, *but some did affirm her as the women's candidate*" [emphasis added].[3]

Just one month before the Southeastern Jurisdictional Conference convened, Rev. Kelly's almost 102-year-old mother died. Kelly attended the Conference grieving her mother's death and finding the jurisdiction as resistant to her election as they had been in 1980. She was not going to be elected in her "home" jurisdiction, despite the deathbed prediction of her mother saying: "Teenie, you are going to be a bishop!"[4]

The Flyer reported:

> From the beginning Leontine Kelly's support—and her opposition— were joyfully and painfully clear. Failing to win the endorsement of her Virginia delegation, she came as an independent candidate to Lake Junaluska, NC, site of the Southeastern Jurisdictional Conference. There she was denied access to delegation meetings and interviews. "There was a sense in which I was never really considered a candidate in my own jurisdiction, except by the clergywomen," Kelly said.

With 330 needed to elect, Kelly garnered 86 votes on the first ballot. But with the unchallenged tradition of vote-trading and block voting among the jurisdiction's three largest conferences, there was no way for an independent candidate to do the floor work and brokering necessary to accumulate votes.

After receiving 43 votes on the sixth ballot, Kelly withdrew from the Southeastern jurisdictional elections Wednesday afternoon with a gracious and prophetic speech. Few could have foreseen at the time that it was also her farewell to the jurisdiction.[5]

Earlier, Kelly had received a phone call from Rev. Barbara Troxell and other women in the Western Jurisdiction, who were meeting at their conference in Boise, Idaho. Convinced of Kelly's gifts for the episcopacy, the women of the California-Nevada Conference had earlier sought and won annual conference endorsement of Kelly as an episcopal candidate, and Kelly was receiving votes on each of the ballots. The women in the West asked Kelly to travel from Lake Junaluska in North Carolina to Boise, Idaho, where she could meet with and be examined by the delegates there. They were convinced Kelly would be seriously considered for election.

Kelly took a day to pray and consult with women supporters in the Southeast. Together they sought guidance and wisdom for what she should do. Finally, on Wednesday evening, along with one of her major supporters from the jurisdiction, Rev. Dr. Diedra Kriewald, Kelly left the Southeastern Jurisdictional Conference and boarded a plane for Idaho. After numerous plane changes, she arrived in Boise early Thursday morning.

By the time Kelly arrived, the Western Jurisdictional Conference had already chosen the first of the three bishops to be elected: Bishop Roy Sano, a Japanese American clergyman and theologian. Rev. Elias Galvan, a Mexican American pastor was receiving significant support from the jurisdiction, as were some white male clergy and Kelly. The women of the jurisdiction began accompanying Kelly to the various conference delegations to introduce her and give her the opportunity to become better known by the voting members of the jurisdictional conference, for she was not well known in the region.

27

Rev. Galvan was elected, and there was much celebration. One more bishop was to be elected, and many did not believe a third racial-ethnic person could be elected, particularly a woman and a candidate who did not even reside in the jurisdiction.

The effect of Kelly's presence was felt immediately, observers noted: "Each time she went to a delegation, the votes went up. Her very vision and spirit were electrifying." . . . The clergywomen who had worked so hard for Kelly's election began to relax as the outcome became clear. Kelly herself, throughout the process, had not been anxious. "If it's the will of God that I be elected, nothing can stop it," she told supporters. "If it's not, I don't want it." . . .

With 95 votes needed to elect, Kelly received 94 on the 16th ballot. Conference delegates "went crazy," and one of the white male episcopal candidates still holding 19 votes stood to speak. "I don't want to tell you how to vote," Bill Walker said, "but I'm changing mine."[6]

Rev. Kelly's daughter, Angella Current, arrived late on Thursday afternoon to support her mother. Inquiring about the conference Current heard from an attendee who

shared that he was a minister, and though he had heard stories about the Holy Spirit, he had never actually felt its presence. He smiled as he repeated how Leontine Kelly had responded to the delegates' questions about her calling to the episcopacy, proclaiming that if "God didn't want her to be elected, she didn't want to be a bishop!" He then admitted that it was during those moments that, for the first time in his life, while listening to her, it happened. He felt the Holy Spirit! "Did she get elected?" [Current] asked. He clapped his hands and said, "Yes! Praises be to God!"[7]

Kelly was the second woman elected to the episcopacy of The United Methodist Church and the first African American woman. She truly believed "if God wanted me to be a bishop, nothing would stop me."

Her election came only slightly more than 24 hours after her withdrawal in the Southeastern Jurisdiction. A visiting group of high school youth, who had felt compelled to delay their scheduled departure in order to be witness to the unprecedented event, spontaneously began singing "We are a Rainbow." . . .

For some, the whole process was sobering. "It was frightening to see how tightly organized these women are," one man said. With the recognition that no white males had been elected to this traditionally white male position came awareness of a new direction in church leadership and politics. One female pastor reflecting on a conversation with a particularly devastated and angry man said: "I can't believe how they (the white males) think the episcopacy is theirs; as though it was taken away from them."

Kelly, responding to those who questioned the wisdom of a completely ethnic episcopal election, cited the UMC's missional priority, the ethnic minority local church. "It is time," she says, "to give recognition and position to authentic leadership. There were many, many years when there were no options besides white males. I am excited at the coalition of ethnic minorities and women and the readiness of the jurisdiction to accept this witness to the rest of the country."[8]

Two years later, following an address by Bishop Kelly at the 1986 World Methodist Conference held in Nairobi, Kenya, South African Bishop Desmond Tutu commented on Kelly: "I would like to give you one very good theological reason why women ought to be ordained, least of all made bishops. It is Bishop Kelly. She was superb. . . . She really made men understand why women say that when God created man she was experimenting!"[9]

Judith Craig

Meanwhile, to the east in Duluth, Minnesota, another election process had been taking place at the North Central Jurisdictional Conference. Bishop Matthews could serve in an active role in the episcopacy for only four years because of church restrictions. She would retire at the end of August 1984, and in addition to replacing her, three others were to be elected in the jurisdictional conference.

Reverend Judith Craig, clergy member of the East Ohio Conference, had resisted the encouragement of colleagues and others to make herself available for the episcopacy. She had served as a pastor and Christian educator, and was currently the director of the annual conference ministries (Conference Council director). Earlier, some had hoped she would be open to ministry as a bishop, and she had received some votes at the 1980 conference in Dayton, where Bishop Matthews had been elected. But after Bishop Matthews' election, Craig found she was less inclined to pursue the office. "My heart is in the local church," she was saying. "Given my druthers, I'd pastor a church."[10] As Craig explained to *The Flyer*, there were

> two major turning points in her decision to become an episcopal candidate. First, the individual voices that had been telling her, "we want you to run for bishop, we want to vote for you," had become a chorus. "People I had always admired and respected were advising me to run. I had always preached God's guidance comes from trusted advisors. So maybe I needed to heed those voices."
>
> Second came the stark specter of the lone [4'11"] female figure seated among the more than 100 active and retired bishops on the General Conference stage. "I sat there as a delegate on the floor in front of the Council of Bishops and felt a depth of commitment to keeping a feminist presence in that Council. I hadn't realized I cared that much. And if I cared, and was willing to urge other women to run, I had to be willing myself."[11]

"Never, never," she said to herself, "must that Council find itself without an active woman bishop in its midst." And so, she returned to her delegation and said, "If you still want to name somebody, I'm sort of willing." The East Ohio delegation endorsed her as their candidate to be considered at the 1984 North Central Jurisdictional Conference.

Craig said that she arrived at the Duluth Conference at peace with her decision.

It was that peace—and the confidence that radiated from it—that both hindered and aided Craig in her episcopal quest. From the outset came questions about her style, her large, confident gestures, her "aggressive, take-charge manner." Women wondered if she really shared feminist values of collegiality and cooperation. Men felt intimidated and overwhelmed by this obviously competent and confident woman.

But it was also that confidence and competency that won her votes.... "She absolutely converted people, she was so good," said one observer. "When faced with questions, she was phenomenal. The process worked better for her than for any other candidate, because her abilities and competencies came out in her responses."[12]

Yet Craig says the jurisdictional election was for her "a kind of hell." The women's caucus was initially kind but not totally supportive. They had gone on record as supporting the election of two racial-ethnic minority men as well as Leontine Kelly. From the beginning, Craig had placed in the top five vote-getters. Recognizing her consistent vote getting, the caucus finally called her in for a luncheon meeting on Thursday, and, according to Craig, confronted her. Their message, she says, was one of concern: "We're not sure you're a trustworthy feminist," she heard. Then, according to Craig, they "grilled" her.

It was the first time Craig had met with a group of all women. She told the group how good it felt to finally stand among them, and how grateful she was to be there. And she responded to still troubling questions about her administrative and personal style.

"Women were wondering whether I would be truly consultative and collegial or whether I would be an autocratic leader," Craig said. The questions took her by surprise, for she perceived herself as collegial and vulnerable. "I learned a great deal about the kind of image I project. I don't perceive myself as an authority figure at all." And yet it was apparent that others did, and that for both women and men (often for very different reasons) her manner might be problematic.

"Maybe because I went to Duluth sure of myself . . .," Craig speculated. "Confidence is harder to take in a woman, and a 'young' woman at that," she says, alluding to other questions about her relatively young age (47) and the 20 years she would have to serve as a bishop.[13]

Craig says she was rather distressed by the encounter, but with the airing of the reservations and hope for the election of another woman to the Council of Bishops, Craig and the caucus left their meeting committed to working together. And all of a sudden, little yellow ribbons (symbol of the women's movement in the church) began to appear on delegates in Duluth with "201" (Craig's number to be used on election ballots).

On Thursday evening, over dinner, word arrived at the North Central Jurisdiction that the Western Jurisdiction had elected Leontine Kelly. The election of Kelly brought a new worry to Craig supporters. Craig herself wondered if she could now withdraw and rest in the knowledge that another woman had been elected to the Council of Bishops. Questions of whether one woman was enough in the Council arose. Craig's supporters urged her to continue in the process.

By Friday afternoon, three men had been elected in the North Central Jurisdiction: Woodie W. White, an African American pastor and denominational executive; along with David Lawson and Rueben Job, both white males. Job had been elected in the middle of the afternoon on Friday. Craig had been a significant vote getter from the beginning and was consistently in the top five. By dinner time, the jurisdictional conference had almost ground to a halt in a stalemate between Craig and another white male candidate who, because of age, would have only four years to serve. Balloting continued and continued, with delegates singing hymns while votes were counted by hand.

Craig remembers there was a time that Friday evening when it was suggested that she and the man with whom she was contesting go out in the hall and decide who was going to be elected and who would announce their withdrawal. Craig resisted the suggestion. "This jurisdiction must decide who it wants as one of its leaders," she said. "We will not make the decision for them." Colleagues and friends encouraged her not to withdraw and to let the jurisdictional conference discern who the person would be to take up the episcopacy.

As the 41st ballot came back to be reported, the Conference was singing "Precious Lord, Take My Hand." Craig recalled the moment,

That's the one song that reminds me of my father. He died in 1980. He was very important to me and would have loved every minute of this. When they walked in with the last ballot, it was as if God said, "Here is the gift of your father."[14]

It was the longest balloting in North Central Jurisdiction history. Judith Craig became the third woman bishop (and the second from the North Central Jurisdiction) in The United Methodist Church.

Celebrations proceeded, and the Jurisdictional Committee on the Episcopacy, the committee whose job is to determine which bishops would serve which conferences in the jurisdiction, went to work. The bishops were to wait patiently to hear from the Committee about their placements. Craig remembers it was nearly 4:00 am when members of the Committee finally came to share with her about her placement to the Michigan area. By then, it was only three hours until a rehearsal for the consecration service and five hours before the service itself.

Rather than going straight to bed for some rest, Craig went to find good friends and colleagues, Bill and Judy McCartney. She asked them to present her to the assembly at the consecration service, and they agreed. Then the three of them decided to go to the shoreline of Lake Superior to watch the sunrise and reflect on all that was taking place. The two Judys had shared a long and deep friendship. McCartney had sometimes even been reluctant to affirm Craig's candidacy because she knew Craig would have to move away from the area in Ohio they both loved. With tears in her eyes on that long Friday evening, McCartney mourned: "I'm losing my friend. I'm losing my friend."

Shortly after six in the morning, the McCartneys and their friend, now Bishop Craig, left the shoreline to find some breakfast and, with no sleep, a required black robe (instead of the new white one that the clergywomen in the East Ohio Conference had given her as part of her preparation for the jurisdictional election process—"just in case"). Sheer exhaustion was coupled with joy-filled expectation as forty-seven-year-old Bishop Judith Craig prepared for her consecration as a bishop of the church. But first, Craig called her mother. Her mother answered the phone with a question, "Is this Bishop Puddinhead?" We need our families, says Craig, to help us keep perspective.

Patricia Broughton, writing for *The Flyer*, reflected:

> Craig's candidacy, more than Matthews' in 1980 or Kelly's, raised issues of sexism and gender identity. Women questioned her feminist commitment and men her non-traditional demeanor. Craig said she sees herself as a "second-wave feminist."
>
> "The first wave is the vocal, visible, attention-getting edge, and then once they get the attention, there needs to be a second wave, equally vocal, not so forceful. I am that second wave. I am very, very aware of the debt I have to my first wave sisters and brothers and appreciative of what they have done."
>
> That woman-identity came across clearly at the jurisdictional conference, participants said. "Craig was saying, ` I'm a woman, the church needs a woman, I'm grateful to have been in a position to develop my gifts,'" [Phyllis] Tholin remarked.
>
> After the election, "everybody felt really proud to be identified with her as a woman," said general agency staff observer Jeanne Audrey Powers. "She proved herself so capable. You don't have to spend energy worrying about how she's getting along. She's comfortable with the authority she has and will give others room to maneuver. I think she'll be a credit to us all. And she knows in a way she didn't know before that her sisters are important."[15]

The elections of Kelly and Craig made 1984 an astounding year. *The Flyer* noted it was also historic in that every United States jurisdiction in The United Methodist Church had considered women as viable candidates for the episcopacy. Kelly, of course, was a national candidate, and she received votes in every one of the five jurisdictions. In addition to Kelly, District Superintendent Deanna Bleyle also received votes in the Western jurisdiction. In the South Central Jurisdiction, Jean Marie Grabher received 74 votes on the first ballot, and in the Northeastern Jurisdiction, District Superintendent Lynne Josselyn ran as an independent candidate. While those three women were not elected, Josselyn said, "I sense we gave a lot of people a vision and a glimpse of the future they hadn't even comprehended before."

Notes

1. Angella Current, *Breaking Barriers: An African American Family and the Methodist Story* (Nashville, TN: Abingdon Press, 2001), 103.

2. Current, *Breaking Barriers*, 104.

3. Current, *Breaking Barriers*, 106.

4. Current, *Breaking Barriers*, 107.

5. *The Flyer*, 6, no. 3 (August 1984): 1, 4.

6. *The Flyer*: 4.

7. Current, *Breaking Barriers*, 108–109.

8. *The Flyer*: 4.

9. Current, *Breaking Barriers*, 116.

10. *The Flyer*: 4.

11. *The Flyer*: 4.

12. *The Flyer*: 4.

13. *The Flyer*: 5.

14. *The Flyer*: 5.

15. *The Flyer*: 5.

1988

SUSAN MURCH MORRISON,
SHARON BROWN CHRISTOPHER

Two jurisdictions had elected women as bishops. Women were emerging as candidates in all five jurisdictions in the United States. The North Central Jurisdiction had elected a woman in 1980 and 1984, and in 1988, two strong candidates were receiving support. Meanwhile, in the Northeastern Jurisdiction, a surprise woman candidate was suddenly lifted up and elected. If the voting delegates were not surprised, the new bishop was.

Susan Murch Morrison

The path to the episcopacy was not a well-ordered one for Susan Morrison. She did not grow up in the church, and many of the traditional expectations for family and church relationships were not hers. She says she "came to ministry through the back door—without the language or some of the things that are traditional in the church. It was through the campus ministry program at Drew University where she began to feel the stirrings of a call. That led her to the Board of Global Ministries' Short-Term Missionary Program, where she became a part of a Brazilian/U.S. team. The team was greatly influenced by the teachings of the Ecumenical

36

Institute, led by Joe Mathews. The time in Brazil was transformational for Morrison. Her lens grew to be that of a global citizen.

Morrison became a pastor and later a district superintendent and then director of conference ministries in the Baltimore/Washington Conference. At the May 1988 General Conference, Morrison was elected to the Judicial Council (Supreme Court) of the denomination. She was the first clergywoman ever elected to the Judicial Council.

Morrison had not planned to attend the Northeastern Jurisdictional Conference, held in West Virginia in July of that year, as she had no particular role there. Her intention was to spend the week at Rehoboth Beach in Delaware where she owned a home. However, the secretary of the Northeastern Jurisdictional Conference called her and encouraged her to attend. Generally, members of the Judicial Council attend conference meetings in their respective jurisdictions. As she was the only member of the Council from the Northeast, the secretary believed it would be good for her to be in attendance. She agreed to drive to West Virginia and be present for at least a day or two.

Packing a bag with some casual clothes and anticipating a relaxed time, Morrison headed off to the conference, where she was promptly seated on the platform with the College of Bishops for the Northeast. Women in the jurisdiction were supporting Rev. Dr. Diedra Kriewald for election to the episcopacy. Kriewald had previously been a major supporter for election of Bishop Leontine Kelly. While Kriewald was receiving votes, there was concern that there appeared insufficient support for her election.

On the third ballot, the secretary of the conference read out the names of all those who had received votes for election to the episcopacy. Morrison received one vote. She wondered which friend was trying to embarrass her! It is typical for a motion to be made, with agreement from the body, that the reading of names stop at either ten votes and above or sometimes twenty. No one spoke up.

The next vote reported two for Morrison. She had just doubled her vote count! The voting process for the day concluded, and Morrison remembers going to bed that night thinking, "Well, I'm glad that's over!"

The following morning, when another ballot was reported, Morrison's votes totaled seventeen, and she began to wonder what she should do. As she prepared to rise from her seat on the platform in order to withdraw, a bishop grabbed her arm and said, "You stay right where you are. Let the Spirit work one way or another. Don't withdraw."

Morrison felt she really needed to talk with Kriewald. "Diedra," she said, "I will not run against you. You're the candidate. You feel called. You committed to this process. You've done the work of preparation. I'm kind of stunned. And I don't think I could possibly be elected."

The two women talked and together they decided Morrison should leave her name in the process. It was time for the church to learn there were numerous women with the qualifications and experience to be considered for the episcopacy. There could and would be times in the future when more than one woman would be available for election within the jurisdiction.

It did not seem appropriate to Morrison to continue to be seated on the platform, as she was receiving votes for election, while all the other candidates were seated on the floor of the conference. She left the podium and took a seat in the back of the room only to hear a delegate from West Virginia rise to ask, "Who is this Susan Morrison? She's taking over the conference. She's like a spirit going through, a wind going through! Is she real? Is she here? Can we see what she looks like?"

Delegations began to want to talk with Morrison. But when they wanted to know what books she had read, Morrison, in her astonishment at what was taking place, says she couldn't remember a single book she had read in the past ten years. She had no vitae sheet to share. She was in shock. A few women, including some who had been leading the work to elect Kriewald, helped prepare an information sheet detailing Morrison's life and ministry. It was a model of women's community and gracious collaboration, says Morrison.

By that evening, Morrison was elected, the only person elected in 1988 in the jurisdiction. Then the shock really set in. It had all happened so fast. She went to her room, uneasy as to where God wanted her to serve. She spent the night worrying, praying, and talking with friends. At one point, the spouse of one of the bishops encouraged her to be open and stay with it. Gradually a sense of peace began to surround her.

At 6:00 a.m., the phone in her room rang. It was Ruth Daugherty, one of the leading laywomen of not only the jurisdiction but of the denomination. Morrison remembers that, as she picked up the phone and heard Daugherty's voice, she felt a calm that said "this will be all right." Daugherty said she and another member of the Episcopacy Committee from Puerto Rico were eager to talk with her. "Come downstairs. And welcome to the Philadelphia Area!" (That area also included Puerto Rico.)

Morrison met with her new colleagues from the Philadelphia Area and then went off to find a robe to borrow because she had not taken one to the conference. One of her strong memories is of the procession into the chapel at West Virginia Wesleyan for the Consecration Service that Saturday morning, wearing her sandals because they were the only shoes she had taken with her. Walking along the aisle, she heard a few whispers of "She's wearing sandals!" (memories of Bishop Marjorie Matthews)!

The night Morrison was elected, clergywomen from across the Northeast laid down their other responsibilities, jumped into their cars, and made their way to West Virginia Wesleyan University. They wanted to be present for the consecration of the first woman bishop in the jurisdiction. In the early morning, they decorated the large statue of John Wesley at the entrance to the chapel with pink streamers. And as people made their way into the consecration service, they gathered around the statue and sang the songs of longing and hope that had been written by women of the Baltimore-Washington Conference.

Morrison's parents were in western New York for the week, attending programs in Chautauqua. It was too far for them to travel to be in attendance for her consecration. But they wondered if perhaps the Methodist House at Chautauqua might have a radio or television that would be broadcasting the events of the consecration of the new bishop for the Northeast Jurisdiction. Her parents walked to the Methodist House on campus and found a man in a rocking chair on the porch. Her mother went up to the man, and said, "I understand there's been an election of a bishop in this jurisdiction." The man said, with a remarkable lack of enthusiasm, "Yes, and it's a woman." Morrison's mother drew herself up proudly and said, "It's my daughter!"

There would be much celebration for her election, and yet, for Susan Murch Morrison, the election called for many adjustments in what was most important in the ministry of the church and in her own personal life. Still, years later she says, "I'd take nothing for the journey!"

Sharon Brown Christopher

Meanwhile, in the North Central Jurisdiction, elections were taking place in DeKalb, Illinois. Three new bishops were to be elected. The jurisdiction was beginning to expect that women had a place in the Council of Bishops, and resistance to considering women for the episcopacy was less palpable than had been the case in 1980 and 1984. More than one woman was receiving votes for election, as were African American and white male candidates. But like earlier times in the jurisdictional conference, the first priority would be to elect a white male candidate: R. Sheldon Duecker.

In the weeks preceding the conference, Charles Jordan, Sharon Brown Christopher, and Sharon Zimmerman Rader (an African American man and two white women) had all been endorsed for episcopal consideration. The three of them had worked together in the jurisdictional Urban Network and on other boards and committees, and each affirmed the others' candidacies. With three to be elected, they knew the conference would be entering new territory to consider electing only women and African Americans. After Duecker's election, it was clear that, at most, only two of the three could be elected. Christopher remembers, "There were some attempts during the conference to discredit the process, and accusations were made that various candidates were signing declarations about controversial theological positions and vision for the church."

Christopher, Jordan, and Rader met and agreed to continue to support one another in the process, to not get caught up in competitive machinations, and to ultimately let the conference make its decision about the remaining elections.

Christopher had been taken by surprise when a clergy colleague approached her nearly two years prior to the 1988 North Central Jurisdiction Conference to alert her to a conversation he and other members of the Wisconsin Conference had been having about her potential candidacy. She had intended and assumed she would be a local church pastor for the duration of her ministry. "Well," she replied, "if you need an answer today, it has to be no. The colleague said, "Yes, we figured you'd say that. So, we want to give you a year to think about it."

Christopher remembers that she was so dumbfounded by the invitation and felt so inadequate for the job that she couldn't even wrap her mind around it. Her first and primary concern was her husband, Charles. She knew that he would support her; that was not the question. But the two were partners in ministry. He was also clergy and, although they worked separately in local churches, she did not want to do anything that might disrupt or diminish his ministry. And no woman who had been elected thus far had brought a spouse with her into the episcopacy.

It took six months for Christopher to even summon the courage to talk with her husband about the invitation from their colleague. As she and Charles were driving down the highway one day (she was driving so her attention had to stay focused on the road ahead), she said, "Charles, there's something I've got to tell you."

"What?"

Christopher told him about the conversation she had six months earlier and what had been asked of her. There was a long pause, and then Charles replied, "Sharon, how long have you been sitting on that? You know, the first day I met you I knew we were going to be having this conversation someday." Christopher says she wasn't surprised by her husband's supportive answer, but "what a gift he gave me." In the coming weeks and months, they spent time reflecting together. And they said to each other at one point: "We've already gone out not knowing, like Abraham and Sarah. We're a clergy couple. We're doing all these pioneering things. Surely God is not inviting us yet another time to step into uncharted waters."

Christopher went through a "huge discernment" process, and carried out conversations with many people. Finally, she went back to her clergy colleague shortly before the jurisdictional process began and reflected with him that, in her ordination, she had given herself to being itinerant and to practicing the spiritual discipline of itinerancy. She had given herself in her ordination to the church, to be assigned where the church wanted her to serve. If the church wanted to assign her to the episcopacy, she needed to pay attention to that request. And so, the process began.

Christopher set one condition to her acceptance of the invitation to be the candidate from Wisconsin. She wanted the whole Wisconsin Conference delegation to pray and discern about electing the best possible people for the episcopacy. The delegation needed to have solidarity about the person they

41

would nominate and support. If, after their discernment process, the delegation determined it was not to be her, then she would stand with them in going in another direction. They agreed to her request. They nominated her for consideration by the jurisdictional conference.

In the midst of this discernment, both of the Christophers faced health challenges. A lot was transpiring in their lives. Two memories of the jurisdictional conference stand out in Sharon Christopher's memory. First, on the last day of deliberation and balloting by the conference, with two elections still to be completed, Christopher awakened and said to her husband, "You know, Charles, today we'll either go back to Wisconsin and serve in ministry, or we'll be appointed to a new place and our whole future will be new. Either way it's a good choice. We can't lose."

Second—almost twelve hours later—Christopher was elected on the 24th ballot. Her election was announced by Bishop Judith Craig, who was presiding at that moment, and she was escorted to the platform to be greeted by her new bishop colleagues and the conference. As Christopher began to walk forward, she turned to look back at her delegation who had been so supportive, and noticed that her place had already been filled by an alternate delegate. But before they approached the stairs to the platform, her escorts stopped in the center of the hall and the whole body came to surround her and hug her and congratulate her. She was surrounded by the community.

"It was such an incredible moment," Christopher remembers. It sustained her for years and years in the episcopacy, remembering that moment of community pressing in and touching and shaking hands and hugging and crying and connecting. There is such power in the response of the community.

1992

ANN BROOKSHIRE SHERER,
SHARON ZIMMERMAN RADER,
MARY ANN SWENSON

"Oops!" It was November at the Council of Bishops' first meeting after the 1992 episcopal elections. Sharon Zimmerman Rader walked into the room where the opening session was to be held, surveyed the room, saw her friend and now colleague, Bishop Susan Morrison, and went to join her at the table. "Oops," was Morrison's response.

Seeing Rader's confused look, Morrison apologized. "Sorry," she said. "It was explained to me (actually I was told) when I joined the Council four years ago that it would be best if the women members did not sit together."

Five women had been elected. Following Bishop Matthews' death, only four women remained to attend Council meetings. Morrison remembers that when women were seen talking to one another, a male colleague observing the conversation frequently would say, "Oh, there are the women caucusing again!" Whenever they joined together, the early women bishops often experienced suspicion from their male colleagues that they must be conniving or strategizing about some kind of change needed in the Council or the church. To minimize the potential threat the men might have been experiencing, the women bishops decided they would not sit beside one another. And yet, says Morrison, "I was aware that we all knew exactly where our sisters were in the room. We could easily find one another because, for the most part, we were in the back of the room adhering to another unspoken expectation for conduct in Council meetings: the newly elected (as well as bishops from non-English speaking countries) took their places in the rear of the room and almost never spoke during the sessions."

Well, almost none of the new bishops spoke up during their early tenure in the Council: Leontine Kelly was an exception. When Kelly heard about the Council's expectations for those recently elected to sit quietly until they had learned what the job was and how to "be" in the Council, she demurred: "I've only got four years of active service in this Council. If I wait for the next quadrennium, I'm done." Judy Craig remembers talking with Kelly about the expectation and acknowledged Kelly, "just kind of broke the pattern and tradition as she proceeded to speak up early and often in the 1984–1988 quadrennium. And while older members of the Council were surprised, they also acknowledged Kelly had something to say, and what she said was worth listening to. She was never shy about doing that." A tradition had been broken in the Council. When new members, including three more women, were added to the Council in 1992, they did not experience as many constraints as had been placed upon their earlier colleagues.

Ann Brookshire Sherer

Ann Sherer's journey to the episcopacy had been shaped by leaders in the South Central Jurisdiction who were increasingly committed to a more inclusive Council of Bishops. In 1992, the jurisdiction was set to elect six new bishops. The clergywomen and a consultation group from across the South Central region wanted to see the new class of bishops include women, blacks, and Hispanics.

"I think it is important to remember," says Sherer, "there are many people who could be elected to the episcopacy. Some of it is the leading of the Spirit. Some of it is politics. Some of it is resentment and personal self-interest. Some of it is strong idealism and great desire for change and a new day. My election wasn't about me. It was about 'we want female leadership.' And the coalition, the women's leadership team, wanted an inclusive group to be elected. Three women from the jurisdiction were candidates in 1992 as well as Alfred Norris (African American) and Joel Martinez (Hispanic). We did press conferences together before the jurisdictional conference. We even did interviews together."

Bishop Alfred Norris was elected first, then Bishop Joe Wilson, a white male from the Texas Conference. Sherer did not expect to get elected; she was from the Texas Conference as well. Although she had successfully pastored congregations large and small in The United Methodist Church, and was the first woman to be a district superintendent in the Texas Annual Conference, the possibility of the South Central Jurisdiction electing two persons from the Texas Conference seemed remote. Margaret Ann Crain was a member of the Missouri East delegation and remembers when Sherer came to meet with the two Missouri area delegations. She heard Sherer's story about growing up and then leaving the Southern Baptist Church, as well as her strong activism in the Civil Rights Movement of the 1960s and 1970s. Crain remembers being excited about Sherer's experience in multicultural settings, "I said, 'Boy do we need this!'" The question remained, however, if the members of the jurisdiction could embrace such a journey as preparation for the episcopacy.

Sherer was the third person elected in the South Central Jurisdiction in 1992, and Bishop Martinez was sixth. Sherer was the first woman to be elected in the South Central Jurisdiction, and the first woman from below the Mason Dixon Line (a pre-Civil War cultural boundary dividing the slave states of the south and the free-soil states north of it). The Women's Leadership Team had worked very hard for the election of Norris, Sherer, and later Martinez, and celebrated the result of their strong commitments.

"I felt claimed," says Sherer. As the coalition had met, done interviews of all the candidates, and strategized how to accomplish their vision, the commitment to be an inclusive delegation and elect new members to the Council of Bishops, who would move the Council to greater inclusiveness, grew. And their work was successful. Six new bishops elected, half of them racial-ethnic or female persons.

It was not until 1988 that central conference (United Methodist conferences beyond the United States) members of the Council of Bishops were full voting members of the Council. Ann Brookshire Sherer remembered that, beyond those with the women, some of her first significant relationships in the Council

45

were with central conference bishops: "Many of us formed quick and close relationships with those bishops who had also been kept from fully participating in the Council. In some ways we were two groups of outsiders: women and the male colleagues from outside the United States. The central conference bishops welcomed us into the community and seemed eager for relationship. They seemed glad when I joined them at the tables. And I soon made several close friendships. My vision of both the church and the world grew."

Twelve years after her election, Sherer was the bishop in Nebraska where a laywoman, Charlotte Reed, who had been part of the 1992 consultation team, resided. Bishop Sherer says she never "saw Reed at a United Methodist gathering or at her local church that she didn't say, "We worked hard to elect you." With her election, Sherer felt a validation of her voice and in her call to the ministry of being an instrument God might use to build a more inclusive church, which grows in capacity to serve all God's people and live in beloved community.

Sharon Zimmerman Rader

Like Marjorie Matthews and Leontine Kelly, Sharon Zimmerman Rader entered ordained ministry as a second career person (former teacher). Rader graduated from seminary in 1976, and was nominated for the episcopacy by the West Michigan Conference in 1988. Her nomination had been a painful one. There were members of the West Michigan Conference who did not believe she had sufficient experience by 1988 to be considered for election as a bishop. Others were convinced her feminism and commitments to full inclusion in the church were not appropriate.

Days before the convening of the West Michigan Annual Conference in 1987, an anonymous letter had been sent to conference members (but not to Rader) by concerned clergy and laity, indicating their grave reservations about her candidacy: she did not have enough experience; she should not be nominated or considered for election by the jurisdiction; she had led only three congregations, and her current appointment to University United Methodist Church in East Lansing, Michigan was acknowledged as one of the most progressive in the conference. Those concerned did not like her theology or her feminism.

Although not a unanimous decision, The West Michigan Conference nominated her for consideration by the 1988 North Central Jurisdictional Conference in DeKalb, Illinois. It was the first time two women had been nominated by annual conferences in the jurisdiction: Sharon Brown Christopher and Sharon Zimmerman Rader. Christopher was elected.

After the 25th ballot at the 1988 jurisdictional conference, Rader had risen to thank the 1988 conference for their consideration of her, and to request she be allowed to withdraw from consideration as a candidate. She recalled the congregation in East Lansing, which had sent her forth the preceding Sunday with a scrapbook full of letters and pictures from children and members alike, affirming her ministry and wishing her well. The associate pastor of University Church had sung a solo that Sunday morning, "In This Very Room," the words of which Rader shared with the jurisdictional conference, as she rose to withdraw.

> In this very room there's quite enough love for all of us
> And in this very room there's quite enough joy for all of us
> In this very room there's quite enough hope and quite enough
> > power to chase away any gloom
> For Jesus, Lord Jesus, is in this very room.[1]

Her withdrawal speech was made in the very same room in DeKalb, Illinois where she had stood to be ordained an elder in the Northern Illinois Conference in 1978. For years, in that conference and then in West Michigan, she had known love, encouragement, and expectation for her ministry. But 1988 was not the time for her election to the episcopacy.

A few short days after the conclusion of the 1988 jurisdictional conference, in trying to make sense of the resistance and contention that seemed to have accompanied her candidacy, Rader and her husband Blaine drove to the Detroit area to consult with her bishop: Bishop Judy Craig. It was a time of healing, self-reflection, and support. Craig remembered her own experience in 1980, when ten people had voted for her as a way to break a deadlock that had occurred between Marjorie Matthews and another candidate. A seasoned colleague from the East Ohio Conference, sitting near Craig, had leaned over and said, "If you want to be a bishop you could do it today. But it's too soon." Craig said she stumbled to the microphone to withdraw.

Rader reflects that in the months and years following the 1988 jurisdictional conference, she came to understand that, in 1988, there had been "too much Sharon Rader," too much believing others' projections about her future, not enough servanthood, not enough trust in the wisdom of the church to determine what and who it needed in its leadership. Morrison's election had been a complete surprise; Kelly was elected by a jurisdiction not her own. Matthews, Craig, Christopher, and Sherer were elected the first time they were nominated. The church knew Rader needed to wait, to reflect, to deepen spiritually, and to grow in expertise.

By 1992, women clergy and other supporters in West Michigan and elsewhere, again encouraged Rader to make herself available; Rader agreed, but this time with a "holy indifference" to the outcome. She was even more committed to the church: the community that had supported her into and through the years of her ordained ministry. She believed, "Whatever happens will be the will of the church. And the church, Christ's body, will be okay. I was calm through the whole process. And I did not hide what I cared about or who I was. I was a feminist, a supporter of full inclusion for members of the LGBT community, and a worker for justice."

All the jurisdictional conferences in the United States meet during the same days, although in five different locations. In 1992, the South Central Jurisdiction had elected all six of its new bishops before the North Central Jurisdiction had even elected one of the three they needed. Shortly after the South Central Jurisdiction completed its work, Donald Ott was elected in the North Central Jurisdictional Conference, meeting in Adrian, Michigan. Charles Wesley Jordan was elected some ballots later. Sharon Zimmerman Rader was the third and final person elected. Again, she was in a place, Adrian, where her journey in ministry had been nurtured. First UMC in Adrian had voted to recommend her as a candidate for ministry. Her two children were born in the local hospital there. She had taught school in the community. The jurisdictional conference was held at United Methodist Adrian College, where Rader's husband had been a professor early in his ministry. Adrian College's Herrick Chapel was the site of the consecration of the three new North Central Jurisdiction bishops. Bishop Edsel Ammons—one of Rader's seminary professors and her first bishop when she returned to Michigan to pastor—preached the ordination service. The community and the connections were precious to her and reminded her of who she had been and who she was becoming. She was the fourth woman elected in the North Central Jurisdiction. For four quadrennia, the jurisdiction had elected a woman bishop at each of its meetings.

Mary Ann McDonald Swenson

The Western Jurisdictional Conference concurrently meeting in Las Vegas, was balloting to elect one new bishop. The Western Jurisdiction is large in geography but fewer in members than the other four jurisdictions in the United States.

The Pacific Northwest Conference in the Western Jurisdiction had a history of nominating a favorite son each quadrennium. Their favorite son in 1972 had been Jack Tuell who was elected, but there had not been another favorite son from Pacific Northwest elected since that time.

Mary Ann Swenson had led the Pacific Northwest Conference delegations to General and Jurisdictional Conferences in 1988 and 1992. By 1992, Swenson says "I was the favorite *son* only I was a *daughter!*" Nominating Swenson was what the conference wanted to do, but she was not certain it was the right moment for her. She had finished a term as a district superintendent, and had been sent to be the pastor of one of the largest churches in the conference. "And that," says Swenson, "really was my heart and soul. I knew myself as a preacher and as a pastor. I had a vision for that place. I loved that place. I loved our teamwork. I knew what we were going to do for the next twenty years. It was just a great place to be. So I was wrestling in my discernment. I really didn't want to be a candidate, but I did want us to elect a woman in the West. Bishop Kelly had retired in 1988, so we didn't have an active woman in our College of Bishops."

Swenson agreed to be a candidate, although she did not think she necessarily needed to be the woman who would be elected. Beverly Shamana was also a candidate and began to receive a significant number of votes until finally, Shamana told the conference, "I just cannot do this." The jurisdiction began to reassess who it was they needed as part of their episcopal leadership.

49

Following the completion of each day's work at the conference, Swenson had been calling her mother, who lived in Mississippi, reporting to her on the activities of the jurisdictional conference. On the next to the last evening of the conference (when all the other jurisdictions had completed their elections), Swenson returned to her hotel room to once again call her mother. Her mother did not answer. Swenson was a bit worried. A few moments later Swenson's hotel phone rang, and it was her mother. "Mother, we've been trying to reach you. Finally, you are home. It's late in Mississippi. Where have you been?" Swenson inquired.

"Well," said Swenson's mother, "I'm down in your lobby. My friends told me I had better get out to your conference. So I flew to Las Vegas." Swenson and her husband went down to the lobby, got her mother, and brought her up to their hotel room, which fortunately, had two beds in it!

"Oh Mother," Swenson said. "There were only five votes for me, but this is wonderful that you're here. We're so happy you're here."

The next morning things began to change. "And," says Swenson, "pretty soon I was a bishop! I wasn't expecting that. I hadn't taken a robe because I wasn't going to do this. Jeff was in shock. After they ushered Jeff and my mother to the front to present us, Jeff said, "I couldn't believe you could open your mouth and say something, Mary Ann. I couldn't even stand."

Swenson remembers that, earlier on the day of her election, as the votes for her began to increase, she had asked her husband if it was going to be okay with him if her election happened. Jeff replied, "Well, I guess it'd be okay as long as we don't go to Denver." The Jurisdictional Committee on Episcopacy assigned Bishop Mary Ann Swenson, second woman elected in the Western Jurisdiction, to the Denver Area.

Swenson recalled her deep grief in facing the reality that, once elected, she was going to need to leave the church where she had been serving. She remembers weeping because she did not want to leave the congregation. Bishop Calvin McConnell, her bishop in the Pacific Northwest Conference, gave her a great gift; he went with Swenson to her congregation the Sunday following her election and introduced her to the congregation as a newly elected bishop of The United Methodist Church. And McConnell left his shepherd's crosier with her for the remainder of the month in July and into August, a symbol of her new office as bishop. "While you continue with the congregation for the remainder of the summer, you will be their pastor *and* you will be a bishop of the church," McConnell said.

Swenson says everyone cried that Sunday morning after her election. But when she left the congregation on the first of September, the congregation gave her a new crosier as a going away gift. To this day, when the carrying of a crosier is appropriate for Swenson's participation in worship leadership, she carries the crosier the Seattle, Washington congregation gave to her.

Note

1. "In This Very Room" words and music by Ron & Carol Harris. Copyright 1979 Ron Harris Music (ASCAP). All rights reserved. Used by permission.

1996

CHARLENE PAYNE KAMMERER,
SUSAN WOLFE HASSINGER,
JANICE RIGGLE HUIE

The year 1996 was tumultuous in The United Methodist Church. Protests during the General Conference led to arrests. The division in the denomination over whether gay and lesbian persons could be ordained or married was widening. Those supporting inclusion were frustrated with the church's stance. The Southeastern Jurisdiction elected its first woman bishop. And two jurisdictions elected a second woman to their College of Bishops. Perhaps the glass ceiling was cracking.

Charlene Payne Kammerer

Charlene Payne Kammerer was the first clergyperson elected by the Florida Annual Conference to the 1996 General and Jurisdictional Conferences. No clergywoman had ever been elected to lead the delegation from Florida prior to this. She believes it was a sign to those in Florida as well as others in the Southeastern Jurisdiction that persons from the Deep South were changing their perspectives on women's leadership in the church.

Kammerer had been a local church pastor, assistant minister to the University at Duke Chapel, and a district superintendent, and knew that most members of the Florida delegation were supportive of her and her ministry. Across the conference were laywomen, clergywomen, persons of color—African American, Haitian, and Hispanic—and many white males who had participated in her election to the Florida General Conference delegation.

But there were also a number of Florida delegates who did not believe it necessarily followed that she should be considered at that time for the episcopacy. Over the years, Kammerer and others in the Southeast had watched as the jurisdiction had refused to consider women with experience and gifts, who would have been strong additions to the Council of Bishops, especially Bishop Kelly.

The jurisdiction and her conference had historically frowned on caucus advocacy work on behalf of non-white, non-male candidates for the episcopacy, and so the collective work of those supporting Kammerer had been carried on "under the radar." However, the circle of people supporting Kammerer for election in 1996 was intensely, but quietly, organized.

The jurisdiction had a process for getting to know potential candidates from across the region. While attending the General Conference, delegates from the Southeast joined together over lunch a number of times to hear from the eighteen or nineteen persons who had been offered as potential candidates for election to the episcopacy.

The 1996 General Conference met in Denver, Colorado, and on the day in May when Kammerer and others were to share their ministry journey and vision for the church at the jurisdiction luncheon, newspapers across the United States carried an article about fifteen bishops of The United Methodist Church who broke "the silence," stating their hopes and commitments on the matter that was "hurting and silencing countless faithful Christians" in the lesbian and gay community. The "Denver 15" (as they came to be called) called for "equal rights for homosexuals, including the right to be eligible for ordination as pastors."

The General Conference and the Council of Bishops erupted in anger, confusion, and (some) affirmation of the statement. As Kammerer remembers her interview luncheon that day, she was the "only candidate" who was asked to respond to the Denver 15 statement. (In fact, she believes she was the *only* candidate from the Southeast during the whole week who was asked.)

Kammerer responded to the question asked of her regarding homosexuality: "I remember saying that I would support the position of the church in regard to human sexuality, but that I was open to the possibility that we, as a church, could change our mind at some point in the future. I said I believed that God made us all equal in creation, that we were all created in God's image. It was like throwing a nuclear bomb in the room. But I said it, and I sat down." And as she left the luncheon and reflected on her statement, she came to believe there was no way she would be elected.

Two months later, in July, the 1996 Southeastern Jurisdictional Conference convened as usual at Lake Junaluska, and had seven bishops to elect. It was an extraordinary number, and those who had continued to support Kammerer's candidacy thought perhaps this was the time for election of a woman to "sneak in." But in light of her General Conference luncheon statement regarding LGBT persons, other clergywomen began to emerge, one receiving considerable votes on the first ballot. "There were some across the jurisdiction who were so opposed to the possibility of my election that they scrambled to find women who, for them, would be acceptable. Those women had never gone through the process and never made the speeches, but they had authentic, good, and effective ministries. The strategy was to split the vote among the women so none of us would get elected. There was organized, in-your-face, resistance to my election every day of the jurisdictional conference."

There was, however, also support for her election. To those who assumed that, if she was elected, no one would accept her for leadership in one of the conferences of the Southeast, the Western North Carolina Conference delegation said, "We want her." That conference's delegation worked very hard to support Kammerer and encouraged other delegations to do likewise. Western North Carolina Conference made it clear it was ready and willing to receive her as their episcopal leader.

Kammerer was the third of seven bishops elected in the Southeastern Jurisdiction Conference of 1996, the only woman in the jurisdiction's group of seven new bishops. She was the first woman bishop with children yet at home and in school.

Kammerer remembers the service at Lake Junaluska where she was consecrated. Each newly elected bishop selects two sponsors to accompany her or him when being presented to the worshiping community. Kammerer selected her two best friends, both women. There had never before been even one woman as a sponsor for a new bishop. Kammerer's election "was a big rupture in the Southeast" and it would be eight more years before another woman would be elected in the region.

Susan Wolfe Hassinger

Meanwhile, in the Northeastern Jurisdictional Conference, four new bishops were to be elected. Among those who entered the conference with the support of the annual conference in which they had served were two candidates from the Eastern Pennsylvania Conference: Alfred Johnson and Susan Wolfe Hassinger. With much courage, because it had never been done before, the Eastern Pennsylvania Conference had determined both Johnson and Hassinger evidenced the gifts and grace needed for the episcopacy. Johnson was African American and Hassinger a white woman. Hassinger remembers that the annual conference and its delegates to the jurisdictional conference had been very "intentional" in their decision to bring two candidates for election.

Johnson was elected first, early in the jurisdictional balloting. Hassinger thought to herself, "That's it; there is not a chance." But she stayed in the election process, not because she thought she might be elected but, "because I had concerns that I wanted to be able to share."

During our 2017 interview in Dallas, another woman bishop (and candidate at the 1996 Northeastern Jurisdiction Conference, Jane Allen Middleton) was reminded by Hassinger of a difficult, yet remarkable conversation the two had following Johnson's election. The hotel room in Dallas where the interview took place became a holy place as the two women talked together:

Hassinger:	Jane, do you remember what you said to me after Alfred (Johnson) was elected?
Middleton:	No, I don't.
Hassinger:	My dear beloved friend and colleague, you came to me and said, "I think you ought to withdraw."

Middleton:	Did I really?
Hassinger:	You did. Because you were a candidate also.
Middleton:	No.
Hassinger:	And I think it was because Alfred was already elected, and he and I were both from the same conference.
Middleton:	Out of the same conference.
Hassinger:	Jane, it was your statement suggesting I withdraw that caused me to have this inner sense of "I hear what you're saying, but God is telling me something else." And so my family and a couple from my first church, who were there supporting my candidacy, went away for lunch. And during that lunchtime it seemed all that came together, and the first ballot after lunch I was elected. I had a peace about it that I did not have before that. Your comment/question to me was crucial in my making the shift.
Middleton:	Wow. I have no memory of that. Although I do remember you saying to me, "Jane, I have a passion for this work."
Hassinger:	That's okay.

The Northeastern Jurisdictional Conference elected two African American men, a white woman (Hassinger) and one white male in 1996. Hassinger was the second woman to become a bishop from the Northeastern Jurisdiction.

Janice Riggle Huie

Janice Huie was not the first woman elected in her jurisdiction. As she reflected on the elections of women before her, she noted, "I think you all have carried a heavier burden. And there's been a bigger price to be paid by those of you were the first in each of the jurisdictions. I'm grateful that you all paid it. The difference you made is significant for not only those of us who came after, but I think for clergy women in every annual conference in those jurisdictions."

The South Central Jurisdictional Conference needed to elect only one new bishop in 1996. Ann Sherer had been elected in 1992, and there were some who thought the work of inclusion in the jurisdictional College of Bishops had been accomplished. Further, "The word was that this would be an absolutely crazy time to try for another woman to be elected, with only one to elect. And (some thought) I wasn't old enough; I was forty-nine, not yet fifty, and our jurisdiction didn't like electing people who were young."

The Women's Leadership Team had played a major role in the election of Bishop Sherer in 1992. There had been an "incredibly wonderful celebration." Huie had also been a candidate that year (when she was even younger!) and the Leadership Team had been supportive of her candidacy as well as Sherer's. Once Sherer was elected, however, Huie believed the jurisdictional conference was "done" with electing women bishops in 1992, and she withdrew from the process.

But the Women's Leadership Team had "tasted success" in 1992, and in 1996, they continued to believe Huie embodied the gifts needed for episcopal election. As she pondered making herself available a second time, she remembers thinking: "Okay, I know everybody's telling me 'You can't do this, Janice. There's only one to elect. You're too young.' But there was a sense kind of whether it's God's timing or whatever, that for me . . . it was a fork-in-the-road kind of time in my life. And I either needed to be elected or I needed to be clear that I was going to be a pastor for the remaining years of my ministry."

Among the "communion of saints" Huie names as significant "mothers of us all" is Joanne Miles. Miles, a laywoman, chaired the Women's Leadership Team in 1992 and 1996. Miles worked with great purpose to enlarge the vision of the church to include women in leadership. Huie remembers that Miles was able to "pull together the support of laywomen, as well as clergywomen who saw her throughout the jurisdiction as an advocate, friend, and colleague. And she could rally the support of United Methodist Women. Her support for Ann Sherer in 1992 and again in 1996 for me made a big difference."

With only one person to be elected, the balloting process took on extraordinary length for the jurisdiction. In addition to Huie and several white male candidates, there was an African American pastor, Rhymes Moncure, who was receiving significant votes. The votes in the jurisdiction just kept getting split among the candidates, with no one getting sufficient support for election.

By the third night of the conference, Huie remembers going to bed with the thought she was not going to be elected. As the conference began again the next morning, "an extraordinary moment took place as Moncure went to the microphone and withdrew. I had absolutely no idea what made him withdraw. I had never spoken with him about withdrawing. . . . The whole conference was astonished. People said to me, 'Did you make him withdraw?' Well, obviously I can't make anybody do anything, and I certainly did not make Rhymes withdraw. But once that happened, people had to decide: where were they going to shift their votes? It was really tough for some folks, bless their hearts. I mean it was really tough for them to think that we were going to have *two* women in the college. There was a lot of conversation about that. In the end, I was elected. It was sort of shocking even to me." Janice Riggle Huie was elected a bishop of The United Methodist Church on the 16th ballot of the 1996 South Central Jurisdictional Conference.

2000

BEVERLY J. SHAMANA,
VIOLET FISHER, LINDA LEE

Eighteen new bishops were elected to the Council of Bishops in 2000, five from conferences outside the United States (central conferences). Of the thirteen elected from the United States, seven were African American, and of those seven, there were three women—the only three women elected to the episcopacy that year.

In the spring of 2000, a U.S. black clergywomen's meeting was held. Amid the activities of the meeting there was much conversation about the hope for another African American woman to be elected to the episcopacy. It had been sixteen years since Bishop Leontine Kelly had been elected. One evening, one woman shared with the group a prophetic insight: three black women would be elected to United Methodist episcopacy in 2000. The group heard and pondered. They prayed and prayed. And in particular, they prayed over the women at the meeting who were potential candidates. They "prophesied there would be three and they prayed for three black women."

Beverly J. Shamana

Although she had been receiving a significant number of votes, Beverly Shamana, an African American clergywoman, had withdrawn from consideration as a bishop at the 1992 Western Jurisdictional Conference. Shamana remembers that, soon after the conference in 1992, she and Bishop Kelly, then retired, were together at a meeting, and Kelly questioned Shamana about her decision to withdraw her name. Kelly reminded Shamana it had been eight years since her own election, and no other African American woman had since been considered for election. Kelly was disappointed Shamana had withdrawn in 1992, and she encouraged Shamana saying, "I hope you will say yes the next time." Shamana says, "Bishop Kelly could see further into the future than I could at that meeting."

In 1996, there was only one new bishop to be elected in the Western Jurisdiction, and Shamana did receive one vote on one ballot. The woman who cast her vote for Shamana that year sent Shamana a note to let her know why she had voted for her, "Just to let you know, we're waiting."

By 1998, Shamana felt led to seek out the assistance of a spiritual director to help her discern the leading of the Spirit about her candidacy for the episcopacy. "Over a period of several months, I began to hear the rhythm of my heart and to envision an expanded call to ministry."

> In spiritual hindsight, I can see how God the Artist was uniting various puzzle pieces together, so I could see the bigger canvas drawn by the Spirit about my calling. After nine years of serving in local church ministry, I was invited to join the Conference Council on Ministries as program director for Mission, Justice, and Outreach Ministries. While developing resources and programs for churches, I saw how God could also use more of my music and artistic talents to reach the heart and soul of God's people through the arts. It seemed as though the various parts of my life and ministry came together as one whole and integrated entity. Many groups responded enthusiastically to have their talents recognized and blessed for the work of Christ through my conference ministries.
>
> It was during these years that God's artistic vision opened doors that put my experience and teaching about the connection between art and faith into a book that I proposed to the United Methodist Publishing House titled *Seeing in the Dark: A Vision of Creativity and Spirituality.* After many nights of non-stop writing, it was published in 2001. I believe that those

eight years between the jurisdictional conferences in 1992 and 2000 were a special time of running (more like sprinting) with the Spirit that prepared me to answer a second call to the episcopacy if offered. Just prior to leaving for annual conference in June of 2000, another Spirit gift was offered in the form of a large conference on Art and the Spirit just blocks from the Conference Center in Pasadena. In addition to truly inspiring artwork, I attended a lecture on Hildegard of Bingen. As I listened through tears, her journey erased any misgivings I had about the next steps on my journey. A final house gathering of women pastors, gifts of symbolic turtles, and laying on of hands, cleared my eyes so I could sing from the heart, "Here I am, Lord. I will go, Lord, where you lead me. I will hold your people in my heart."[1]

Because of that inner journey and [those] helpful conversations, I came to the California-Pacific Conference with a clearer vision and a readiness to follow God's footsteps wherever they would lead on this unpredictable spiritual journey. Having finished the final chapter of my book, and with the support of the annual conference, I arrived at jurisdictional conference and read a statement on the unfolding of my journey and the steps I had taken to solidify my readiness as a candidate.

Shamana did not want to ignore her withdrawal eight years before, and the faith the conferences had put in her at that time.

She recalls, "I think when I shared my statement with the jurisdiction, there was something about delivering it that felt like it was not just a statement on paper. . . . I felt a response from the conference that was more than just listening. I felt that they were talking back to me even in silence."

The 2000 Western Jurisdictional Conference took the nominating ballot, identifying potential candidates. Shamana was among those identified. The conference then took its first ballot, and Shamana was elected. A long-time clergywoman friend and lay delegate, Becky Haase, went to Shamana, and said, "Don't you think you ought to call your mother, Beverly?" Her mother arrived as quickly as possible, on a plane from Los Angeles to Casper, Wyoming, and so did her future husband, Walter Woods. Shamana was the second African American woman elected to the United Methodist Council of Bishops. Both Shamana and Kelly were elected in the Western Jurisdiction.

Violet L. Fisher

Other jurisdictions were also considering African American women at the 2000 jurisdictional conferences. In the Northeastern Jurisdictional Conference, Violet L. Fisher, an African American woman who had been reared in the Pentecostal tradition, was receiving more and more votes. Bishop Susan Morrison remembers the affirmation for Fisher, which began "on the first ballot, and it just kept moving, kept right on moving."

As in the Western Jurisdiction, only one vacancy needed to be filled in the Northeast in 2000. When votes for her kept mounting, Fisher says she did not know what to do. She went to her bishop, Susan Morrison. "I'm so nervous," she said, "I don't know what to do." "Just be still," said Morrison. Fisher remembers she felt as though she had butterflies, but inside her spirit was saying, "Just say yes."

Fisher's journey to the episcopacy was unique. Her formation, she says, comes from the church. "My pastor said that he saw gifts in me. I was given positions and responsibilities that many persons my age had never experienced (and even persons who were older had not experienced). I was kind of pushed out into leadership."

Fisher's father belonged to the African Methodist Episcopal Church, but her mother belonged to a Pentecostal denomination, the King's Apostle Movement. Violet was the first woman ordained in her mother's denomination, and her ordination spoke volumes; of all the women in the Movement, she was the one who went to college.

Violet heard the call to preach at the age of sixteen. She loved preaching (and still does) and believed her life would be one of going from place to place to preach. Her mother, however, insisted that she had to go to college. "You're going to go to school somewhere," she told Fisher. "You're not just going to preach. Violet, you're not going to make a living preaching."

Fisher tried to tell her mother that she was not going to go to college. Her mother insisted. And since her older sister Clemente had become a teacher, Fisher became a teacher. She also became the secretary to the bishop of her Pentecostal church for a number of years, which helped her to "understand how the episcopacy works."

Other women leaders in the King's Apostle Movement were older, but they did not go to school or get a college degree. Fisher was the first female in the Movement to graduate with a master's degree in education. "I just kept right on pushing, and they just put their arms around me and groomed me."

With her education completed, Fisher became a teacher in the black, segregated schools on the eastern shore of Maryland. When segregation was struck down by the Supreme Court of the United States, she was chosen to be one of the teachers to move to a mixed-race school. "I always wanted to learn and to do, and I wanted to be in the know. All that helped me in later years," said Fisher.

Fisher had not been teaching long when she attended a meeting where a missionary presented a slide program with stories from Kenya. Fisher was convicted by the presentation and decided she must go to Africa. Her parents had many reservations about such a radical change in her life, but Violet just kept saying "I'm going; I'm going."

Fisher went to talk with the principal of the school in which she was teaching. "Would you hold my job for me?" she asked. His reply was that he could not do that, but that they would try to find something for her when she came back. "Well", said Fisher, "I'm leaving. I'm going to Africa when school closes." "By yourself?" her principal and other teacher colleagues wondered. "Yes," replied Fisher. "I saw a slide presentation, and I've got to go."

Fisher remembers leaving from Dulles Airport in Virginia. Her father, whom she had never seen cry, was crying. "I've got to go," she told him. "Violet, why?" her father implored. "Why, Daddy? I don't know why, but I have to do it." Fisher went off to Kenya for the summer, returned to the U.S., and taught until she could get her money and life organized, then took a sabbatical from teaching and returned once again to Kenya, where she stayed for four years in the bush with the Kikuyu people.

The King's Apostle Movement had made Fisher their international evangelist, and when she was yet in her twenties, had put her in charge of overseeing women's work in the Movement. But she says she had a deep longing to return "home" to the church of her father, the Methodist Church. "I wanted to go home, and they (the Pentecostals) wouldn't let me go." Finally, one of her best friends, a United

Methodist pastor in the Baltimore-Washington Conference, Alfreda Wiggins, called and said, 'Vi, it's time for you to come back home.' And that's when I made the move—that very year."

Fisher went off to further her theological education and was ordained in The United Methodist Church. Her first United Methodist appointment was in urban ministry in the city of Philadelphia—another cause for concern in her family, as she was the only one of the six children in her family to ever live in a city. Utilizing all her past experience and her teacher training, Fisher began a tutorial program and an after-school program, and the congregation started a feeding program close to the church. She loved the ministry she was doing there. But after a few short years, the bishop, Susan Morrison, had another idea. She asked Fisher to become a district superintendent on her Cabinet.

Fisher felt the work at the church in Philadelphia was making a difference in that part of the city. Asked to be a superintendent, Fisher wasn't so sure she wanted (or was ready) to leave the congregation. She worried about what would happen to the African American congregation she was serving. Morrison said, "Vi, pray about it. Just pray about it." And Fisher says she prayed and came to affirm, "Yes, this is an opportunity for me as a black woman to do this, not only for the church, but for my people."

There were some in the Eastern Pennsylvania Conference who were not pleased with Fisher's appointment to the Cabinet. She had not been a United Methodist very long. She had not served multiple congregations. She was African American and a woman. Fisher says she heard and felt the pain of those who believed they had been neglected while she was chosen. "But," she says, "I had somebody [Morrison] who was being led by the Spirit to ask me to do this. And that settled it with me. So, I didn't go around with a guilty feeling like 'I took your place.' I accepted the invitation as a God thing."

When Fisher's nomination to the episcopacy came in 2000, she heard some of the same concerns: "She just got here" (to The United Methodist Church). As the jurisdictional conference process began, she felt "nervous, scared to death." She does not like to be rejected, and did not want to experience failure. She could not sleep.

Early one morning at the conference, "one of my friends came. She knocked on my door and said, 'Vi, I came to have prayer with you.' My whole family was at the conference, too—all my siblings and my dad. They came, and they were saying, 'We're praying with you and for you.' The African American sisters had a prayer vigil, and they anointed me and laid hands on me; they prayed and prayed and prayed through the night for God's will to be done. And I had people who were calling me from all over because I'd been an evangelist and had preached everywhere. They were calling me, saying 'we're hearing what's going on and we're going to be in prayer for you.'"

Fisher says she had butterflies in her stomach during the jurisdictional process, "but in my spirit, I was just saying, 'God, whatever your will is, whatever your will is.'" Fisher was the only bishop elected in the Northeastern Jurisdiction in 2000.

Linda Lee

Linda Lee had not taken seriously the comments made by colleagues and friends over the years that she might one day be elected a bishop. Tallulah Fisher, a clergy member of the Northern Illinois Conference, was the one many expected to be the first African American woman elected in the North Central Jurisdiction. Lee was fine with that possibility and thought Tallulah would be a wonderful bishop.

But Fisher suffered a heart attack and died in the summer of 1999, and the conversations about the election of an African American woman in the jurisdiction changed. Lee's bishop, with whom she was serving as district superintendent, Bishop Don Ott, mentioned to Lee in the fall of 1999, that there was talk of her as a possible episcopal candidate for the 2000 elections, since Fisher was no longer living. An active member of Black Methodists for Church Renewal (BMCR), she was also encouraged to run by persons in that caucus. A pastor who had the spiritual gift of prophecy offered the insight that Lee would soon hold the "highest office of the church." Lee was the chair of the Black Clergywomen of The United Methodist Church at the time; another prophetic insight had been given in that group that there would be three black women elected to the episcopacy in 2000. This combination of things, along with the earlier reflections about this possibility throughout her ministry, encouraged her to make herself available for consideration at the 2000 jurisdictional conference.

Lee says she felt like, "Mary, pondering it in her spirit and taking it under advisement and all that. I talked to my husband and, some days, was ready to say yes to the possibility, and other days I wasn't so certain. At the May General Conference of 2000, I had decided to back out, but it was the black clergywomen who convinced me to stay in the process."

Lee also had a conversation with Bishop Leontine Kelly about her potential candidacy. Lee says Kelly "encouraged me to go forward. If she had said anything that had given me an indication that maybe it wasn't a good idea I would have quit then. I can't remember her exact words; I just remember that she was very affirming. She was a real foundation for me. She had been part of the church in Cincinnati my first husband's family had been from. She knew their family and was a compassionate counsel when needed. I valued what she had to say." Most of all, Lee prayed, asking what God wanted her to do.

At the North Central Jurisdictional Conference, held in July 2000, however, Lee was told by supporters from BMCR that "it wasn't quite yet my time." Early in the conference, Gregory Palmer, an African American man, had been elected. She wondered if the conference would decide they had elected the African American person for the quadrennium and not be open to the election of a second black person. Besides, before the conference, she had been told what some African Americans were saying: "She needs to straighten her hair." "She needs to change the way she dresses." "Too much Afro-centric clothing and accessories." "She needs to step back and wait until the next time."

After the encouragement and endorsement of the Black Clergy Women of The UMC the previous spring, Lee remembers praying to God: "The only way I'm going to know if this is really your will or not is if I stay in it. And so I decided then not to back out. And I told God (I do *tell* God things sometimes!), 'I'm only doing this once, because it's the only way I'll know if it's Your will.' I put God to the test."

"What I knew," says Lee, "was that I needed to stay focused on what I understood I would do if it happened: to continue to work for racial and other forms of justice in the world and in the church, missions, to preach the gospel, to speak on behalf of those who could not speak for themselves, to continue to work for unity in the church and the world, to bring hope and healing to those who needed it. These things had been part of my life and ministry for decades. The vote before I was elected was when I felt something like a cosmic shift. That's when I knew it was happening. It was like five votes or something away from an election. And then it happened; the vote was taken and Bishop Jordan and Bishop Ott came to escort me from my place to the platform. It was an amazing spiritual time for me."

Lee says she knew when she looked back on it, there were many people she had relationships with since her days in West Ohio, when she was "working on ethnic local church concerns, missions, and working with women's groups and BMCR, ecumenical work in the communities where I served, serving as vice-chair of the Board of Ordained Ministry, serving as a delegate to General Conference and serving as a district superintendent. I realized how many people I knew in almost every conference of the jurisdiction and all of the relationships that had been there over the decades of my whole ministry. All of those connections came flooding into my awareness, and it felt like they all came together in that moment. And there was no doubt that—through all these people over the decades and at the jurisdictional conference—it was God's doing. The experience was . . . it was an amazing spiritual time for me." In 2000, Lee became the first African American woman elected in the North Central Jurisdiction.

It had been sixteen years since Leontine Kelly, the first African American woman, had been elected to the episcopacy of The United Methodist Church. With the election of Shamana, Fisher, and Lee (the *only* women elected in the 2000 jurisdictional conferences), there were now four women of color in the Council. It would be another sixteen years until more African American women would join the Council of Bishops.

Note

1. Dan Schutte, "Here I Am, Lord," *The United Methodist Hymnal* [hereafter, *UM Hymnal*] (Nashville: United Methodist Publishing House, 1989), 593.

2004

HOPE MORGAN WARD, DEBORAH KIESEY, JANE ALLEN MIDDLETON, MARY VIRGINIA TAYLOR, SALLY DYCK, MINERVA GARZA CARCAÑO

2004 was a remarkable year too, but in ways quite different from 2000. The first Hispanic woman was elected. A woman who was quite clear about her commitment to inclusion of LGBTQ folks (Sally Dyck) was elected. The Southeast elected more women. 2004 was the largest class of women elected to the Council of Bishops up to that point.

Hope Morgan Ward

Bishop Hope Morgan Ward recalls thinking, "What have I done? We've left our life, really left our life. But does anyone ever know what lies ahead? We don't know where we are going. We don't know what awaits us. Yikes! Jurisdictional conference of 2004 was a tremendously hard week, for sure. It wasn't so much about the rounds of interviews and having people ask me about hot topics; it was . . . the end of the old and the beginning of something else . . . whatever that means, wherever that means, with whoever that means. The uncertainties were one hard place to inhabit."

For Ward, the suggestion of serving in the episcopacy came in a variety of ways. In response, she and her husband Mike prayed, meditated, and conversed with wise spiritual friends. Engaging especially with the stories of women in the Bible, she found grounding. And pragmatically, for Ward it came down to four questions:

1. Do I have the experience necessary?
2. Do I have the gifts needed?
3. Am I available to go?
4. Am I called to it?

Ward had been a local church pastor, a conference director of Connectional Ministries and a district superintendent. She had worked closely with the bishop, experiencing vicariously the day-to-day work. She felt she had the experience to do the work and the gifts that would be needed. Her husband was supportive, and their children were in college. They could be available if elected. She had a hard time gaining clarity about the fourth question of calling to the episcopacy.

In 2003, the Southeastern Jurisdiction clergywomen held a consultation at Lake Junaluska, North Carolina. Ward traveled with a small group from her North Carolina annual conference. The other women anticipated the support and encouragement that would be present at the gathering. The looming episcopal elections were not part of their expectations, and there was no conversation in the car about General and Jurisdictional matters or elections of bishops.

There were others at the consultation, however, who were eager to talk with Ward. As she walked down a hallway at the retreat center, Ward was stopped by two clergywomen from the neighboring Western North Carolina Conference who emerged suddenly from a meeting room. They asked her to come into the meeting room. Ward entered the room full of Western North Carolina clergywomen indicating their support for her as a candidate for the episcopacy.

Surprised, Morgan Ward responded, "We don't do this in our conferences." "Well, we do now," said the women from Western North Carolina.

Ward remembers the encounter as "an amazing moment. I never expected someone from the neighboring conference to begin this conversation with me."

Ward told her gathered sisters about her thoughts, reflections, and hesitancies around the fourth question. "Am I called to the episcopacy?" A woman in the group suggested, "Perhaps this is a part of your call." The women gathered around Ward, laid hands on her, and prayed for her. This was a powerful moment, pivotal in her discernment to let the candidacy process unfold.

Another personal factor loomed large; she did not want to "leave home." Ward loved what she was doing in ministry. Her husband was engaged in important and wonderful work as superintendent of Public Instruction of North Carolina. She loved her colleagues. She loved her friends. Her household, parents, siblings, nieces, and nephews either lived, or often gathered, at the family farm or on the coast of North Carolina. She thought about her aging parents and valued proximity to them, having the prescient sense that, "if I leave North Carolina, I will be far away when my father departs this earth (and indeed I was)." The hard task was to entrust all this to God.

Ward was the second woman elected in the jurisdiction, eight years after the first woman, Bishop Charlene Kammerer, had been elected. She was assigned to the Mississippi Conference, which was a "long way from home." Ward likes having roots: "I had always thought I did my best work where I had strong roots, connection, friendship, history. I was sent to lead in a place (Mississippi) where I did not know one soul other than two people who I knew from a General Conference committee."

On the long drive to Mississippi in late August 2004, Ward and her husband Mike practiced saying, "In Mississippi, we . . ." Leaving behind their work and connections in North Carolina, they were Mississippians now. Ward was wonderfully welcomed by the Mississippi Conference. The Episcopacy Committee encouraged her to "go home whenever you need to."

She remembers it as a huge stretch, not without homesickness, starting from scratch with people and churches and an unknown annual conference culture. Yet the experiences of a United Methodist lifetime and of ministry across thirty years, the support of her family, spiritual connections near and far, and new opportunities for expansive growth and service were all serendipitous, sustaining, and life-giving.

Deborah Kiesey

Deborah Kiesey hates cameras and does not see herself as an "out-front" person. She is quiet and thoughtful, and because of increasingly debilitating effects of childhood polio, her mobility is severely decreased. Yet the Iowa Annual Conference had experienced her strong and effective leadership as pastor and district superintendent, and affirmed her for consideration by the 2004 North Central Jurisdictional Conference. Kiesey says, "I really didn't expect to get elected, but I thought, 'I trust the judgment of my Iowa colleagues, so I'll just go and see what happens.'"

Early in the 2004 North Central Jurisdictional Conference, held in Dubuque, Iowa, Hee-Soo Jung was elected, and there were two more elections to be completed. As Kiesey's votes continued to rise, a respected colleague went to her and encouraged her to withdraw her candidacy. The colleague was a strong supporter of Sally Dyck, and did not believe the Conference would elect two women. Dyck had been a candidate the prior quadrennium, and the expectation by many was that 2004 was "her turn" to be elected. "It needs to be Sally," said the colleague, "We can't elect two women."

Kiesey remembers getting a bit irritated, thinking, "What difference does it make whether we have two women and one man or two men and one woman elected?" Kiesey continued on in the election process, but she needed to engage the process according to her own particular needs. Going from delegation to delegation, answering questions, and presenting herself to many different people was exhausting; to stand for any length of time was very tiring.

Kiesey made the decision to break tradition and simply move from one place to another with her crutches or electric wheelchair and then to sit, not stand, as she conversed with delegates who wanted to know more about her and her vision for the church. "To be honest, I think that made a difference. It felt like it was more just kind of an eye-to-eye conversation." Kiesey's vote numbers kept increasing, and she remembers her husband Brad saying to her, "I think you had better think about all this. It's really going to happen." Kiesey says, for her, it was the first time she really began to think about the possibility that she could be elected, and what an annual conference or the Council of Bishops would do with somebody who used crutches as much as she did. Just getting around was going to be an issue.

Kiesey believes her diminished physical ability opened many eyes across the church to the need for greater accessibility for all people. One worshiper at an annual conference ordination service shared with her his unhappiness with her for not standing through the hymns in worship, until he realized the ordination service was lengthy and physically demanding even for someone without special needs. Churches across the conferences she served began to be more aware that they were not as accessible as they had perceived they were. "Oh," they would report before she arrived to preach, "We're accessible," only to discover they had six steps up to the chancel and three more into the pulpit. That hasn't necessarily been my goal, but it has been what's happened over the years as I lived and ministered with people and congregations."

It surprised Kiesey that the North Central Jurisdiction elected her a bishop of the church. She was the second person elected in the North Central Jurisdictional Conference in 2004, the sixth woman elected in that jurisdiction. She was assigned to the Dakotas Area to begin her episcopal ministry. Driving from Fargo, North Dakota down the interstate highway to Sioux Falls, South Dakota, early in her episcopacy she remembers thinking, "Oh my God, I'm a bishop! It was absolutely that clear. And there wasn't a panic. In fact, there was a peace that actually was a part of that. But it was just, 'Really? Me? Just me? I'm Deb. I'm just me.' Who would believe that I would be able to be part of all those great people (in the Council of Bishops) that I've always read about and heard about? I don't belong there. It took a long, long time to feel like I belonged."

Jane Allen Middleton

Jane Allen Middleton remembers that, following the 1996 Northeastern Jurisdictional Conference, when her candidacy had not been affirmed, she began to enter into some years of serious and deep discernment. She came to understand that, in 1996, she "didn't really want to be a bishop. I just wanted to be elected." Her annual conference, New York, had endorsed three candidates in 1996, and to Middleton, it seemed the delegation and the conference's candidates were "just all at odds. There was a measure of dysfunction going on, not just in the conference, but within me as well. It was not a healthy thing. But you know, in all of this it feels like God has God's way."

Middleton was elected three times as the first clergyperson delegate to General and Jurisdictional Conferences: 1992, 1996, and 2000. Acting on her discernment, coupled with the fact she had served only one year as a district superintendent, as well as the jurisdictional conference's need to only elect one new bishop in 2000, Middleton had not been a candidate in 2000.

Once again elected to lead the New York Annual Conference delegation to General Conference in 2004, Middleton recognized because of the denomination's age restrictions for bishops, she would now only be able to serve as a bishop for four years. Her age and past experiences with her annual conference, and in the 1996 episcopal election processes, seemed to limit the possibility of being elected in 2004. "But the more I thought about it, the more I thought, 'Well, maybe so.' I had served in leadership at all levels of the church, chair of the Conference Board of Ordained Ministry and the Council on Ministries, member of the General Council on Ministries, district superintendent, conference staff responsible for Spiritual Life Programming for Laity and Clergy. More importantly, I felt a nudging from the Spirit to share my love of God and enthusiasm for the potential of the church, which had nurtured me all my life."

The New York Annual Conference did not endorse Middleton in 2004; they chose another candidate. Middleton felt the annual conference's decision shut the door on her possible election, and she was hurt. But she says, "There was just something in me that was saying, 'Maybe you need to be open.' I went on a silent retreat, and one of my purposes for going on that retreat was to enter into a time of discernment. And I had a very profound dream in that time that really felt like it was a message to at least deal with the possibility of becoming a candidate. I also got a call from somebody in another conference saying, 'We've been thinking about this. And some of us want to support you. Would you be willing to have your name put into nomination?' And so, I decided to do that, to allow my name to be put into nomination should I receive enough votes to qualify as a candidate. I went to the 2004 Northeastern Jurisdictional Conference not endorsed, but then I was elected! And it did feel very right. I remember waking up on Sunday morning after election thinking, 'Well, when I grow old I shall wear purple!'"

Mary Virginia Taylor

Although not mandatory by church law, if a person is to be considered as a candidate for the episcopacy, it has generally been important to have been elected (and elected early) by their annual conference to be a delegate to the General Conference. Mary Virginia Taylor, like Bishop Middleton, had been elected by her annual conference to the General Conference in 1984, 1988, 1992, 1996, 2000, and 2004.

Dindy Taylor's experiences in ministry were varied and deep. As one of the early clergy couples in the Holston Conference, she and her husband Rusty had shared ministry, parenting, and life together. Through the years she had served as a college chaplain, an associate pastor, a local church pastor, and a co-pastor with her husband. Within the conference, she had been the chairperson of the Board of Ordained Ministry, the chairperson of the Council on Finance and Administration, and the chairperson of the Personnel Committee for the Council on Ministries. On the general church level, she was elected for eight years to the denominational General Council on Ministries, where she served on the Advance Committee with Bishop Judy Craig, and she was elected for another eight years to the General Board of Church and Society, where she chaired the Joint Seminar Committee. She was serving her sixth year as a district superintendent in 2004. She reflects that she has "had so many incredible experiences in ministry beyond the local church and has been blessed beyond anything I deserve."

After the death of Bishop Cornelius L. Henderson in 2000, the Southeastern Jurisdiction held a called-jurisdictional conference in 2001 to elect his successor. Taylor was one of the candidates considered at that time, but early in the voting, she rose and withdrew her name from consideration. By 2004, the Holston delegation was interested in supporting her for the episcopacy, yet she wondered, "Am I brave enough to do this?" Reflecting on the blessing of the annual conference and on the many opportunities she'd had to serve in ministry, she began to question, "Why has God blessed me so much? Is it time to give back?"

As Taylor and her husband began to explore a response to the conference's invitation to become their candidate, Rusty supported her and cautioned, "If you do this, do not chicken out and withdraw too soon. You hang in there and let the process unfold."

Taylor went to the 2004 Southeastern Jurisdictional Conference as one of two episcopal candidates from the Holston Conference. She remembers someone warning her that the Southeast Jurisdiction will never elect two women, and if they do, it will not be two white women. Hope Morgan Ward was elected on the first ballot of the conference, but there were six bishops to be elected from the Southeast in 2004. Annual conferences in the jurisdiction were each committed to one or more candidates, and the jurisdiction was "very divided on who it wanted to elect." The balloting continued for an unprecedented length of time, and yet Taylor's delegation held steady in support of her: 20 ballots, 25, 26, 27. Delegations were locked into support of their favorite daughter or son, and the jurisdictional conference appeared unable to move toward election.

Taylor gathered in the chapel with the Holston delegation and told them, "You don't have to continue to vote for me. I release you from supporting me. It's okay." With that, the Holston delegation prayed that God's will would be done. One friend asked her if it was okay if they continued to vote for her anyway. After that time together in the chapel, for reasons Taylor does not fully understand, her vote totals began to rise. On the 33rd ballot, Taylor was elected, the seventh woman bishop who was part of a clergy couple. She was the sixth bishop elected in the Southeastern Jurisdiction in 2004—but not before the jurisdiction "ran out of printed ballots before the voting was finished!" They announced that there were no more printed ballots and pieces of paper would be distributed. One of her friends whispered to her husband, "What happens when they run out of paper?" After her election, Bishop Marion Edwards shared with Taylor that he could see the Holy Spirit moving throughout Stuart auditorium in her election. One of her clergy friends told Taylor he believed that her election would probably mean the "end of Rusty's ministry."

Taylor had not been at all convinced before arriving at the conference at Lake Junaluska that she would be elected a bishop. She did not want to assume anything, and had not taken a clergy robe with her to use in case of her election and consecration as a bishop. She had also made plans to participate in a mission trip to Willow, Alaska, led by her husband Rusty with members of his congregation the week following the jurisdictional conference. One seasoned bishop advised her that, since she had been elected to the episcopacy, she would need to cancel her scheduled mission trip to Alaska; while another bishop instructed her that one bishop "cannot tell another bishop what to do." Taylor's daughter packed the suitcases for the newly elected bishop of The United Methodist Church while Taylor went to borrow a clergy robe from the local Cokesbury store at Lake Junaluska and prepared for her consecration as a bishop. Following the conclusion of the jurisdictional conference in 2004, Taylor departed for the mission trip to Alaska!

Taylor says she has never wanted to "interact with people as *I am the bishop!*" There have been ways in which she resisted assuming the role. She illustrated that with a story of a time in Estes Park, Colorado, when a woman took a picture of her carrying her own luggage to the car because the woman thought it was so "cute" that a bishop would carry her own luggage.

Sally Dyck

Sally Dyck, also part of a clergy couple, had been a pastor and district superintendent in the East Ohio Conference. Her family had raised her in the General Conference Mennonite Church. Dyck attended Boston University and transferred her membership to The United Methodist Church as a young adult. Her commitment to personal piety and its connection to peace and justice advocacy remained strong, and she was ordained an elder in 1981. She continued to be a strong advocate for full inclusiveness in the church.

In 2000, the General Conference was held in her "home" conference, East Ohio, and she had been very active in speaking and acting on behalf of those who did not yet know full acceptance in The United Methodist Church. "People were saying to me, 'You know, you should run for bishop.' I didn't take that (the bishop part) seriously, but I thought, 'Okay, jurisdictional conference could be a platform to kind of keep the conversation about inclusiveness going. I will go and will allow myself to be on the ballot a time or two, and then I'll be able to just get out. Being in the process, I'll be able to message and keep the conversation going about inclusiveness."

The first ballot of the 2000 North Central Jurisdiction Conference was taken, and Dyck found herself a front runner. Surprised and without a fully developed core of supporters who would work on her behalf to secure the election, her vote totals went up and down. Dyck stayed in the process, but eventually was not elected in 2000. "But," she says, "I know it was a good thing."

Dyck describes the years following the 2000 process like living with "a target on your back." People were watching her—her leadership, her ministry, her witness. As she lived from 2000 to 2004, she entered into a time of discernment, a time to "really think about what this would mean in terms of my own calling and situation, as well as for my husband." She continued to advocate for full inclusion of the LGBTQ community in the church.

Finally, Dyck "just put my name in there again and (waited) to see what would happen. It was a bit of a hurdle process. There was a mantra at the 2004 North Central Jurisdictional Conference that seemed to say 'Anybody but Sally.'" Eventually, after 36 ballots, Dyck was elected. She believes there were some people who were disappointed in her election. "Be careful what you stick your toe into!" Dyck warns.

Minerva Garza Carcaño

During the 1996 General Conference, Rev. Jeanne Audrey Powers had invited Minerva Carcaño to join her and two other women clergy from the Minnesota Annual Conference (Rev. Kathy Austin Mahle and Rev. Patricia Toschak) for dinner one evening. In the middle of their dinner, the Minnesota women told Carcaño they had been in a prayerful time of discernment and they believed God was calling her to the episcopacy.

Carcaño was forty-two years old and had never thought about the episcopacy. She was quite shocked, humbled, a bit confused, and had all kinds of questions about what it would mean for a clergywoman from the Rio Grande Conference in the South Central Jurisdiction to be considered for election as a bishop in the North Central Jurisdiction. Carcaño remembers finishing dinner and saying to the three women, "You know, if nothing happens, the fact that you three think that I could do this is a blessing. I need to pray about this and figure it out." She also remembers walking back to her hotel room and thinking, "This is not something I can discern by myself."

Desiring advice and consultation from those who knew her best, Carcaño asked for a meeting with the Rio Grande General Conference delegation. Members of the delegation were people who had been her mentors over the years. They were people she respected deeply. The Rio Grande delegation was all men save for one laywoman, Dalila Cruz. Carcaño shared the invitation she had received from the women at the Powers dinner. The men heard her out, asked many questions, and were very polite as Carcaño remembers the meeting. But she also remembers feeling patronized.

Finally, one of the men said to her, "You're too young." Carcaño admitted she probably was. But Dalila Cruz was not happy with the assessment. Carcaño remembers Cruz "just kind of rose in her spirit and leaned on the table to say, 'Wait a minute. You all started running men when they were only thirty-eight. So why is Minerva too young?' She pushed them." After some more dialogue, the delegation told Carcaño they were in support of this opportunity for her.

Wanting to fully disclose her new possibility, Carcaño determined she would share further with members of the national UMC Hispanic Caucus (MARCHA) Executive Committee. Accompanied by Cruz, Carcaño discovered the committee had already heard about the possibility of her candidacy and encouraged her to be available. A Hispanic man was also a candidate for election in the North Central Jurisdiction, but the Executive Committee said, "You need to run. Why is it that people, white people, can run four or five or six candidates? Why can't we run two Hispanics? You each have different gifts, different abilities, different ways of approaching ministry. Why can't there be two?"

Carcaño talked with her spouse. She talked with her mother, who was a deep spiritual guide for her. And she talked with her daughter, who was still very young. "Do we get to travel some more, Mama?" her daughter inquired. Carcaño told her daughter yes, and the immediate response was, "Let's go!" With the affirmation and reassurances she received from family and community, Carcaño called the Minnesota clergywomen and agreed she would be available to be considered as a candidate in the North Central Jurisdiction in 1996.

Carcaño was a delegate to the 1996 South Central Jurisdictional Conference, which was held in Kansas City. The conference had begun and was proceeding when she received a phone call from Austin Mahle, telling her she had received ninety votes in the North Central Jurisdictional Conference, and people were becoming more and more interested in her candidacy, but they were confused because there were *two* Hispanic candidates in the jurisdiction. The women in the North Central Jurisdiction wanted Carcaño to come to the North Central Conference. Again, Carcaño gathered members of her own delegation, as well as others from across the South Central Jurisdiction, to assist her in determining next steps. They talked and prayed and talked and prayed some more, from 11:00 p.m. to 3:00 a.m., seeking discernment. Finally, at three o'clock in the morning, they encouraged Carcaño to go to Indiana to the North Central Conference, talk with the Hispanic man there who was also receiving votes, as well as other candidates, and discern next steps. At 5:30 the next morning, Carcaño was on a plane. She was greeted by women from the North Central Jurisdiction and, at her initiative, immediately met with other women candidates from the jurisdiction. She also reached out to the other Hispanic candidate, who told her he would not meet with her one-on-one, and informed her that she was being called to meet with the Hispanic caucus of the jurisdiction.

The leaders of the Hispanic caucus in the North Central Jurisdiction were not happy with her appearance at the conference. Calling her to a meeting with them, they began to challenge her presence in Indiana and the support she had been garnering: "Who do you think you are being here? We don't know you." There would be an attack and then a refusal to allow her to respond. "You have no right to speak here," they told her.

In retrospect, Carcaño was grateful for the experience, for she learned about commitments and perspectives that were "not the church that I thought we should be cultivating. It wasn't the community of Hispanic leaders that I thought we should be. It opened up some conversations later, the fact that this kind of thing happened in our community all the time because we competed against each other, and we allowed the system to use us against each other as well. And we could see all the system and layers of racism that get internalized and that we just take in and react against each other, rather than against the racism and the sexism of a system. So, I went home and processed it. I realized that it was a gift that people would think that I could do this, that I had the gifts, particularly from those women and then from those men who began to say, 'I was wrong to say you couldn't run.'"

The Rio Grande Conference and the South Central Jurisdiction began to have different conversations with Carcaño between 1996 and 2000. The Rio Grande Conference wondered why a conference other than her own should be supporting her candidacy. And so, in 2000, she became the candidate of the Rio Grande Conference, and also received support from the Women's Leadership Team of the jurisdiction.

Still, there were hesitations and withholding of support. Carcaño experienced the ambivalence of her own Hispanic community as they began apologizing for her: "Well, yes, she is a woman. Yes, she is pretty radical." Plus, the Women's Leadership Team that had helped to get two white women elected in earlier conferences failed to put together the pieces to aid her election.

Most devastating of all was the character defamation and character assassination. First, Carcaño was accused of being a terrible mother for running for election with an eight-year-old daughter. A few hours later, the rumor being spread was that she was a lesbian with a husband and a child as a "front." And then there was the leading clergy member of one of the conferences in the jurisdiction, who talked to other delegates, telling them Carcaño was "Satan incarnate; she will destroy the church."

A friend and close spiritual companion took Carcaño aside and said, "There is evil here. Are you sure you want to continue submitting yourself to evil?" Just a week before the 2000 conference, Carcaño had a dream where she felt she was hearing the voice of the Holy Spirit saying to her, "You will face evil, but I will be with you." Carcaño told her friend, "God is with me. And I need to be faithful."

Carcaño went through a long period of depression following the 2000 South Central Jurisdictional Conference, not because she was not elected, but because of the character defamation. The depression lingered and lingered, and she kept trying to figure out how to find internal peace again.

In February of 2001, within a period of ten days, Carcaño received invitations from three different bishops from three different jurisdictions in the U.S., inviting her to consider transferring membership to their annual conferences to engage ministry in a new place, with new people. By the time she received the third call, from Bishop Edward Paup inviting her to transfer to the Oregon-Idaho Conference, where he would appoint her to be a district superintendent on his Cabinet, Carcaño thought, "Okay, Lord, are you trying to say something to me?" Carcaño consulted with her own bishop in the Rio Grande Conference, who granted her permission to transfer. She decided she needed to make a clean break, leaving both her annual and jurisdictional conferences because, "I won't be healed; I won't be free for leadership if I just simply leave my annual conference."

Moving to the Western Jurisdiction was not totally easy; Carcaño had earlier been receiving votes for election to the episcopacy in the jurisdiction, and she worried they might think she was moving there in order to find an easier place to be elected. If she was going to transfer, it was important to her that it be for the sake of ministry and not to be positioned for an election process, not even for the episcopacy. She talked daily with Paup about the ramifications of her possible transfer, until finally, one evening, in yet another telephone consultation, Paup said to her, "I believe you could be a bishop of the church. But right now, I need you to be a district superintendent in Oregon/Idaho." The conversation convinced her, and she went to the Oregon-Idaho Conference.

In 2004, Minerva Carcaño was elected a bishop by the Western Jurisdiction of The United Methodist Church. She was the first Hispanic woman to be elected to the Council of Bishops and the final of six women elected to the episcopacy in that year. It was the largest class of women elected to date.

2008

ROSEMARIE WENNER, PEGGY JOHNSON, ELAINE J. W. STANOVSKY, JOAQUINA FELIPE NHANALA

If 2004 was a momentous time with the election of six women bishops from four different jurisdictions in the United States, the years 2004–2008 brought even more excitement and change. Four women from four different regions of the worldwide church had been elected by the end of 2008.

Prior to 2004, the central conferences of The United Methodist Church (those regions in Africa, Europe, and the Philippines) had never elected a woman to the episcopacy; and few women in those regions had even seen women in large church appointments or serving as district superintendents.

Rosemarie Wenner

Central conferences establish their meeting dates separate from the jurisdictional conferences in the United States. The Germany Central Conference met in 2005. Prior to the opening of the conference in Wuppertal, Germany, the Committee on Episcopacy for the Conference had begun a process of identifying multiple persons as potential candidates for consideration and election to the episcopacy; one person was to be elected.

While the Committee discovered there were many across Germany who thought Rosemarie Wenner might be the best person they could elect, they were not satisfied with bringing only one nominee to the conference. Rather than bringing only Wenner's nomination, the Committee changed an established process and suggested the conference instead have a new process allowing any and all who might be interested or nominated to be considered. Following that open nominating process, each person who received votes would be asked: Are you willing to be a candidate?

The presiding bishop for the Germany Central Conference was Bishop Walter Klaiber. Wenner had been a member of his Cabinet, and he had seen her spiritual and intellectual gifts as well as her skills in leadership. Listening over the months prior to the conference, he too had begun to wonder if it might be possible that Wenner would be the one elected by the central conference. Klaiber invited Bishop Sharon Z. Rader to be present at the conference, where she would lead a Bible study and preside over the election process.

Each person who received votes on the open nominating ballot was invited to speak to the conference and declare her or his willingness to be considered. Nearly all stood to decline the opportunity. Wenner said, "Yes, here I am. If the church calls me, I'm ready to serve. I do not know what it will look like, but I am ready to offer my gifts." One district superintendent who had been nominated said, "I will not say no if you elect me. But I do think that it is time for Rosemarie Wenner to be elected." It took four ballots, and Wenner was elected.

Wenner says, "You really could see some of the struggles some people were having. One of the main questions was always, 'Is The United Methodist Church in Germany ready for a female bishop?' I used to answer, 'How could we know if we don't try?' But also, I was known as *the* female theologian. I was known as someone who really was engaging in the church for equal possibilities for men and women. And that might also have been part of the struggle for some of the rather conservative people. Still, I was elected to be the leader of the whole church, not one faction. Although, I also thought people should know where I come from and where I'm standing."

During our interview, Wenner reflected, "The journey has generally been very positive in Germany. I never expected that it would be that positive. But

83

on that day when I was elected and you, Sharon [Rader], were welcoming me to the Council of Bishops and putting the bishop's pin on me . . . I get emotional remembering that time. But, of course, I then needed to get myself prepared to preach at the Consecration Service!"

It is unheard of in the United States for a newly elected bishop to preach at their Service of Consecration, which is held within hours of the time of her or his election. But that is the tradition in Germany. Wenner says: "You have to prove that you can do it. There was not much opportunity to think about preaching until after I was elected. The text had been determined: Matthew 28, our mission statement so to speak. I had to invest a lot of thought as I prepared for that sermon."

During the conference, Wenner had been staying in the Deaconess House in Wuppertal. The deaconesses of that order are very conservative and evangelical in the sense the Scripture has to be taken, not literally, but very strictly. Wenner saw them as people who were hesitant to support her at the beginning of the election process. "But on the day of my election I returned to the Deaconess House to find on the door of my room a wonderful handmade episcopal sign with the signatures of all the deaconesses, elderly women most of them. They said, 'You are our bishop. We will pray for you.' And that is one example of how maybe 90 percent of the church in Germany responded to my election."

Rosemarie Wenner was the first woman elected from the central conferences (those conferences outside the United States) to the Council of Bishops of The United Methodist Church. She was one of the seven men and women who were elected in the central conferences between 2005 and 2008.

Peggy Johnson

If Rosemarie Wenner's personal journey to the episcopacy looked somewhat traditional (pastor, district superintendent, theologian), the election in the Northeastern Jurisdiction, three years later, of Peggy Johnson from the Baltimore-Washington Annual Conference did not fit a usual mode.

Johnson says, "God has a sense of humor. I was never a district superintendent or a council director. I never served a big church. My whole ministry had been inner city, minimum salary, deaf church ministry for twenty years. Everything was in sign language; I didn't use my voice. All I had to do was sign. If I had laryngitis it was 'a piece of cake.' Babies screamed; who cared? I was identified as someone who understood something about disabilities, so I was always getting myself in odd places doing the inclusive piece for this denomination. That gave me a chance to see some of the working and the politics (of which there are plenty). And because I had those opportunities, I was elected in 2000 to lead the conference delegation to the General Conference."

As the first clergyperson elected to General and Jurisdictional Conferences, Johnson was then elected to be a member of the Northeastern Jurisdiction Episcopacy Committee and had watched and gotten to know many of the bishops in the jurisdiction. She found them to be "regular people," doing the work for which the jurisdiction had elected them.

By 2007, it was acknowledged that Bishop Violet Fisher was going to be retiring, leaving only one woman bishop active in the Northeast Jurisdiction, "a jurisdiction known to be very inclusive," says Johnson. Johnson began getting "God nudges." She heard encouragement to make herself available to run for bishop in 2008, and her responses were "O Lord, send someone else." "No, Lord, I cannot speak; I use my hands." "They won't like this, you know."

Johnson entered into a time of prayer and fasting for twenty-one days to discern God's will for her life and ministry. By the end of the twenty-one days, she still did not feel she had an answer; she wanted "lights or something, some kind of knocking me off the porch."

Ending her time of prayer and fasting, Johnson departed to join an Emmaus Walk gathering. Accompanied by deaf people from her congregation and interpreting for them, she almost immediately encountered another participant who greeted her, "Hello Bishop," At that moment, Johnson says, she simply gave in; "All right, all right. I'm going to run. I will do it." She says at that moment "peace just flooded my life."

Some people just laughed in her face at the possibility of her candidacy. Some people said, "That's silly," or "That's not really true is it?" Johnson would reply, "Yes, it was true." Sometimes she even apologized for the challenge and confusion the possibility of her candidacy made in the minds of those who believed she did not fit the usual mold for one to be considered.

The Baltimore-Washington Annual Conference delegation to the 2008 Northeastern Jurisdictional Conference had a process for determining who they might endorse for the episcopacy that year. When they began their deliberations, there were four women under consideration. Each potential candidate was interviewed by the entire delegation. Johnson received a call after all had been interviewed saying, "We've chosen you. You are the one we will support."

As Johnson remembers the rest of the process, she says, "So, it looked like they were going to vote for me, at least on the first ballot, because that's one of the things they kind of make an agreement to do. So I went to the jurisdictional conference and began participating in the interviews of candidates that are held there, and they went rather well. I feel like I have a warped sense of humor, but it kind of worked for me. On the first ballot, I got the second most votes . . . but then the number of votes I was receiving kept rising. I thought, 'Oh my, I'm in this. I'm going to do this. It's unheard of.'"

"On the 9th ballot, I was elected. It's been an incredible journey, an amazing privilege for these almost ten years now. So that's my story and I'm sticking to it!"

Bishop Peggy Johnson was the fourth woman elected from the Northeastern Jurisdiction and the only person elected in that jurisdiction in 2008.

Elaine J. W. Stanovsky

Elaine J. W. Stanovsky's life has been intertwined with The United Methodist Church since she was a high schooler. Having been sent as a young adult observer to the 1972 General Conference, the Pacific Northwest Conference elected her as a lay delegate and head of delegation in 1976. Stanovsky was developing deep and broad experience in denominational life. Even an Episcopal Church priest who was a family friend had early on recognized that one day, "You're going to be a bishop!"

Stanovsky remembers the priest's acknowledgment of her future potential as something of a burden. She did not want to be worrying about everything she said or did, if that was what it took to be considered for the episcopacy. Stanovsky spent years trying to fend off that expectation for her future. After 1976, she did not return to the General Conference as a delegate for twenty years.

In the interim, she was ordained and entered into ministry. She served on denominational boards and agencies, was a pastor, director of an ecumenical agency, district superintendent, and eventually became the director of Connectional Ministries and assistant to the bishop in her annual conference.

In 2004, when she was director of Connectional Ministries, Stanovsky supported her good friend and colleague, Robert Hoshibata, as a candidate for episcopacy. In spite of her commitment to support Hoshibata, two different people independently came to her office, closed the door, and said to her, "You have to decide what *you* are going to do when you get votes at the upcoming 2004 jurisdictional conference." Stanovsky says the conversations "freaked me out." She would not run against her friend, Hoshibata.

Stanovsky went to the 2004 Western Jurisdictional Conference having decided that, if she did receive any votes, she would honor those who were voting for her and not withdraw, under two conditions: (1) Rev. Hoshibata was no longer in the running, and (2) the balloting for other candidates was deadlocked. After Hoshibata had been elected, and the other candidates had been trading votes back and forth for several ballots, someone handed her a note that read, "You will receive votes on the next ballot. She honored her plan, received votes, and did not withdraw until the deadlock had been broken. Then Bishop Carcaño was quickly elected and Stanovsky "breathed a sigh of relief."

From 1996 to 2008, Stanovsky served on the Jurisdictional Episcopacy Committee and observed bishops from the jurisdiction as they carried out their role and responsibilities in the office. As the 2008 season for electing bishops drew nearer, however, Stanovsky knew she "needed to be clear" about her willingness to make herself available for election. She went to a Catholic retreat center where she met with a spiritual director and shared with her the questions that were filling her heart and mind. In the evening of the first day at the retreat center, the community gathered for prayers. A priest led the worship service and preached on a text from the New Testament book of 1 Timothy concerning bishops. Stanovsky, thinking the spiritual director had betrayed her confidence, packed up her things and left the retreat center that very night.

Continuing to watch and learn from those who might become her colleagues in the Council of Bishops, Stanovsky finally concluded that, if she was to be a candidate, she "needed to demonstrate to myself that I could behave up to my standards and that I act with integrity. I think I did that."

Endorsed by her annual conference and willing to make herself available for the office, Stanovsky went to the 2008 Western Jurisdictional Conference, where two persons were to be elected. Grant Hagiya was elected early. Late that night, there were two women receiving significant votes for the second opening: Stanovsky and Janet Forbes from the (then) Rocky Mountain Conference. During one of the breaks in the conference proceedings, the two women met and talked, acknowledging that "one of us is going to be the other's bishop!" Attention having been given to their relationship and truth-telling to each other, Stanovsky remembers that, after her exchange with Forbes, she simply relaxed into the election process. The 2008 Western Jurisdictional Conference elected Elaine J. W. Stanovsky a bishop of the church.

Joaquina Filipe Nhanala

In Mozambique, the annual conference has a unique (and far less political) manner of nominating candidates for the episcopacy. During a worship service at the annual conference prior to the convening of the quadrennial central conference, members of the annual conference are given the opportunity to write down the names of two persons they believe should be considered for election as a bishop. The ballots are sealed in an envelope and carried to the central conference for opening and reporting there as part of the nominating process.

Joaquina Felipe Nhanala's potential for leadership had been recognized by Bishop Almeida Penicela (Mozambique), who had sent Nhanala and her husband (also clergy) across the continent to Liberia for theological training. When their educational work was finished, Bishop Arthur Kulah of Liberia ordained Nhanala on behalf of the Mozambique Annual Conference. Two women had been ordained earlier in The UMC in Mozambique, but it was ten more years until Nhanala was ordained. She and her husband were the second clergy couple in the Mozambique Annual Conference.

Over the years, Joaquina Nhanala had become known by many across the Mozambique Conference because of her work with World Relief, an ecumenical agency working on HIV/AIDS and youth programming. In addition to her work with that agency, she was the pastor of a growing and vital 1000-member church in Maputo. Still, Nhanala was surprised when her name was read at the 2008 Africa Central Conference as the second highest vote getter in the "nominating ballot."

Nhanala says some of her colleagues had mentioned to her earlier she might be considered. But there had never been a woman bishop on the continent of Africa. The majority of the delegates to the Africa Central Conference were men, and she knew many were hesitant about a woman in leadership.

Nhanala had been "out in the field," where the church was at work on critical issues facing persons and life on the African continent, and she had shown a heart for being where the people are. She was better known than even she was aware. Nhanala says, "When the plan is from God, it happens. There is nothing that can hinder it from happening."

Bishop Linda Lee had been invited to the central conference to be present and preside over the election, but the election process did not take long. Joaquina Felipe Nhanala was elected on the second ballot of the 2008 Africa Central Conference. Bishop Lee preached for Nhanala's consecration service, using a passage of scripture from the first chapter of the book of Jeremiah, proclaiming God had a plan for Jeremiah, and God had a plan for Joaquina as well.

Nhanala's election as the first woman bishop in all of Africa was an historic moment for the continent and for The United Methodist Church. Leaving the site of the Africa Central Conference, Nhanala flew back to Mozambique. Upon arriving at the airport, she noticed a large gathering of people on the tarmac. Security in Maputo was not as rigid as other places in the world, and with few police on duty at the airport, people from her country had gone to the airport, ignored the police, and rushed onto the runway. Looking at the crowd, Nhanala and those accompanying her wondered about the reason for the gathering. "Who's coming to our country," she wondered. Finally, someone clarified for her. They were there for Nhanala—all those people, the press, and the television cameras—were there to greet the newly elected African woman bishop!

But there was more. There is an African tradition that when someone goes away for a long time or comes back from an important journey, the first thing she or he must do (before they do anything else or go anywhere else) is to go to the "hut of their ancestors" to be presented. The Episcopacy Committee had adapted that tradition and were prepared to immediately carry Nhanala off, not to be with her husband and family, but to go to church, the "hut of her ancestors."

Nhanala went, as her friends and colleagues had planned for her, and she says the time was deeply meaningful for her and the Africans gathered that day. They went to the house of God, and there she was presented to the people of the Mozambique Annual Conference. There were prayers for her leadership and for the church.

The reception at the church was huge. For most of the people gathered, there was little understanding of the election process Nhanala had been through or of any of the other activities of the Africa Central Conference. Surprisingly, the person who preached at that homecoming celebration used the exact same text Bishop Linda Lee had used hundreds of miles away when she preached at the Service of Consecration for Nhanala. Nhanala says, "It was just a God thing. . . . Our people are gracious to leaders. There is no doubt there are challenges [in her work as a bishop], but also I feel that warmth, the love from the episcopal area. . . . I repeat often the Jeremiah passage that Bishop Linda Lee and the pastor at that welcome reception preached: God has a plan for me. I believe God's really using me to build up God's church."

2012

SANDRA LYNN STEINER BALL, DEBRA WALLACE-PADGETT, CYNTHIA FIERRO HARVEY

2012 was significant in several ways. Sandra Steiner Ball was elected first in her jurisdiction, before two men. The South Central Jurisdiction had not elected a woman since Janice Huie in 1996 until Cynthia Fierro Harvey joined the College of Bishops in 2012. Debra Wallace-Padgett became the first woman to be elected to the episcopacy from the Kentucky Annual Conference and the first woman to be assigned to the North Alabama Conference, the Birmingham Area. Cynthia Fierro Harvey was the first and only Latina woman elected from the South Central Jurisdiction. Firsts continue to occur regularly.

Sandra Lynn Steiner Ball

Prior to three different jurisdictional gatherings in the Northeastern Jurisdiction, Sandra Steiner Ball had been asked to make herself available for consideration as an episcopal candidate. Twice (in 2004 and 2008) she rejected the invitation.

Although persons in the Northeastern Jurisdiction had begun to encourage Ball to consider the episcopacy, she did not believe she was being called to the office; nor did she wish to leave important ministry in which she was engaged. She had entered ministry "out of a great passion about the importance of the local church, about the church being the place where people could truly find themselves as valued and valuable."

As the years continued, it became clearer that her ministry was not to be located only in the local church. She had been asked to be a district superintendent, which she eagerly accepted "with great enthusiasm, because now my leadership was not just affecting one local church in one community, but I had the opportunity to work with pastoral leaders and congregations to help them discover what they really can do and to help them realize the importance of their place in the community for children, for youth, and for adults who felt that life had passed them by, who felt that they were worthless, and for those who had not found or realized that they were valuable or loved or lovable."

By 2007, she had been appointed to be a leader in the Peninsula-Delaware Conference as the director of Connectional Ministry, yet one more place where she felt called to help the "whole area discover what they could be for all God's children." Approached to consider the episcopacy in 2004, she had said, "No," feeling what she was doing was too important to be interrupted.

Again in 2008, colleagues and delegates to the 2008 Northeastern Jurisdictional Conference asked her to consider making herself available as a candidate for the episcopacy. Steiner Ball says she gave the invitation more consideration the second time around. She prayed about the invitation and thought about it. And the clear message she "got from God was 'not yet.'" Steiner Ball still had children at home. She says, "God gave me my husband and my children as the first gift in my marriage and family. I felt that I was called to see that through, at least through their high school years, before I seriously considered another direction."

Growing up, Steiner Ball was a "differently-abled child" who had great difficulty communicating. Because of her communication problems, she was sometimes called "stupid" and labeled as someone who would not be able to do much in life. Her parents and the church taught her otherwise. She says, "My family talked to me about what I could and could not do. They advocated for me at school and demanded that my teachers acknowledge that I was a child who simply thought differently and processed differently than a lot of other people."

In her local church, as she was growing up, she found acceptance. It was the place where she felt valued and valuable, and where a space was made for her. At the church, she began to learn what she could do. And she learned at the church and through her parents that she needed to take the word *can't* out of her vocabulary and accept the truth that she was not "stupid."

Steiner Ball's acceptance and encouragement in the church developed in her a great passion for ministry, particularly for the local church. She believed she was called to minister with people and lead in a way where she could challenge people to take the word *can't* out of their vocabulary.

The delegates and others with whom she worked in Peninsula-Delaware had observed Steiner Ball's ministry—her passion, her commitments, her example. Again in 2012, they approached her and requested she consider running for the episcopacy. Steiner Ball responded, "No I will not *run*. The episcopacy and the election to the episcopacy is a movement of the Spirit, not something that is a political kind of search or a political kind of game." She did promise to pray, and finally reached a decision to allow her name to go forward to the Northeastern Jurisdictional Conference. Steiner Ball offered a caveat to her willingness to engage the process, "I want to be very clear. I'm not going to do those prep interviews. I'm not going to go around and meet other delegations, because I've got ministry that is important right here where I am. I'm called to this ministry I've got right now. If anything happens, it's going to be a movement of the Spirit."

Steiner Ball went to the Northeastern Jurisdictional Conference in 2012. She had not spent much time in preparation. She did not have a statement to make to the delegations she was to meet upon her arrival. She had been given four prepared questions to respond to as she went from one interview to another, but until she arrived at the conference, she had not given much thought to her answers.

Steiner Ball was rooming at the conference with another clergywoman, Charlotte Nichols, and finally she asked for some help. She said, "Charlotte, these are the questions I'm supposed to answer. I believe this is how I want to answer them." The night before the interviews, she practiced with Nichol's feedback and help.

Steiner Ball says she could not imagine in that process anything worse than having her spouse or other family members spending a whole day accompanying her to the interviews. Still, she needed someone who would go with her into the interview rooms, listen to the questions and her answers, and pray for and with her. Members of the Peninsula-Delaware Conference delegation agreed to support her in that way.

Steiner Ball was the first person elected in the Northeastern Jurisdiction in 2012. There were two others elected in the jurisdiction that year. She was the only woman.

Steiner Ball's family was not in attendance at the conference when she was elected to the episcopacy. "People laugh," she says, "When I was elected, I literally called my husband and said, 'Well, honey, I have something to share with you. I was just elected. So it looks like you and I are going to move. I don't know where yet. You might want to be here for the service of consecration.'"

Steiner Ball's husband agreed it might be important for him to go over to the conference. He picked up her parents, and together they made their way over to the Jurisdictional Conference for her consecration as a bishop of The United Methodist Church.

Bishop Steiner Ball says, "It would have been just fine for me to have stayed in ministry in the Peninsula-Delaware Conference. I loved that conference, grew up in that conference. It was a great ministry. But I couldn't have been more thrilled in terms of my assignment as an episcopal leader to the West Virginia Area, because I do believe that God has me right where God needs me in order to help others discover what is possible, what they *can* do in the midst of many challenges."

Debra Wallace-Padgett

Debra Wallace-Padgett was the first woman to be elected to the episcopacy from the Kentucky Annual Conference, and the first woman to be assigned to the North Alabama Conference, Birmingham Area. She was the fourth woman bishop elected in the history of the Southeastern Jurisdiction.

In 2008, Wallace-Padgett had been elected to lead her annual conference delegation to the General Conference. Tradition in the Kentucky Conference had been that the clergyperson elected to lead the delegation would also be considered as a potential candidate for the episcopacy. Wallace-Padgett chose not to make herself available in 2008. As she weighed the ministry and building expansion taking place at St. Luke's United Methodist Church, where she was serving as senior pastor; her husband Lee's ministry as executive director at Aldersgate Camp and Retreat Center; and the potential impact on Lee and their teenage children; it was clear to her the episcopacy was not something she was being called to do at that time. Leading up to the 2011 elections in her annual conference for those persons who would be delegates to the 2012 General Conference, Wallace-Padgett began thinking, "This is something I ought to settle in my heart. I need to discern whether or not I'm willing to make myself available if I'm elected to lead the delegation again. If I'm not willing to stand as a candidate for the episcopacy, I should make that known, so the conference will be able to discern in the conference's way who they want to elect first, with the ramifications it has."

Wallace-Padgett joined her husband, their two teenage children, and six others on a backpacking trip in the Rocky Mountains in the summer of 2010. During this eight-day wilderness experience, Wallace-Padgett had plenty of time to think, pray, and reflect: "I went into the trip with the full intent of it being a time of discernment related to the elections in the denomination. While backpacking in the Rockies, I discerned that if the Kentucky delegation chose to invite me to do so, I was to enter the episcopacy process. The question confronting me was not, 'Am I called to be a bishop?' It was, 'Am I willing to take the next step in God's calling on my life and become an episcopal candidate?'"

"If the jurisdiction elected me as a bishop, then I would interpret that as the church community confirming that God had called me to the episcopacy. I had no idea what the outcome would be. But God's call to take the next step in the discernment process, if asked to do so by the Kentucky Conference, was really clear to me."

Wallace-Padgett was elected on the 11th ballot at the 2012 Southeastern Jurisdictional Conference. And the journey continues: "I continue to try and simply take the next right step in my journey with God and as a leader in the church. I have learned to trust that, though I do not always see the whole picture, God will make clear to me the next right step to take."

Five persons were elected to the episcopacy in the Southeastern Jurisdiction in 2012. Wallace-Padgett was elected fourth, following the election of three men.

Cynthia Fierro Harvey

Cynthia Fierro Harvey was not endorsed for the episcopacy by her annual conference. There were, however, others in the South Central Jurisdiction who believed she embodied the gifts and grace that were needed in the leadership of The United Methodist Church.

Harvey arrived late to a gathering of clergywomen from across the jurisdiction, only to find the women had been talking about her and her leadership. The clergywomen believed she should make herself available, and they were prepared to support her.

Harvey says, "I never believe that you run for this. For me, if you wake up every day wanting to be a bishop, I think you should not be a bishop. I was not one who had decided I was going to be a bishop. That was just never on the radar for me."

The women were quite insistent about Harvey's possible candidacy. They hounded her. Seeking clarity about the possibility, Harvey invited a couple friends who she considered her spiritual directors to meet for a time of discernment. They met in the basement of a church in a rather clandestine way because she did not want anyone to know what was being contemplated. Harvey and her friends wrestled with questions of faith and ministry: Who am I? Why would I want to do this? And they encouraged her to write and talk about her "I believe" statements (statements she continues to refer to from time to time).

As a result of the time spent with her spiritual director friends, Harvey made the decision to be available to the election process in the South Central Jurisdiction. "In our jurisdiction," she says, "you go through a gauntlet of interviews, even prior to going to the jurisdictional conference. I had a great time in the interviews, got to meet great people. I thought, I've won. I've won because I've met the leadership of the church, and I've had a great experience. Frankly, I entered into the process with no expectation of being elected."

Harvey admits she went to the jurisdictional conference just hoping she would garner enough votes not to embarrass herself or her family. She told her mother-in-law, who lived near to the site of the conference not to come, because she did not expect to be elected. She told her daughter who was in school not to attend (and if she did, to come only toward the end of the week, because she anticipated not being elected without a long struggle).

Harvey led the vote tally on the first ballot. She lost some votes on the second ballot, and she turned to one of the women who had encouraged her to make herself available and asked for advice. "Smile," said her friend, "but not too much." Harvey gives thanks for "the clergywomen who were my encouragers: Gail Ford Smith and some people from conferences other than my own" and acknowledges there were moments of great pain and "a lot of humility that comes with the process."

Cynthia Fierro Harvey was elected on the 4th ballot of the 2012 South Central Jurisdictional Conference, one of the three people elected at that conference and the only woman. Sixteen years had passed since a woman had been elected in the South Central Jurisdiction.

2016

SHARMA D. LEWIS,
SUE HAUPERT-JOHNSON,
CYNTHIA MOORE-KOIKOI,
TRACY SMITH MALONE,
LATRELLE MILLER EASTERLING,
LAURIE HALLER, KAREN OLIVETO

The election of seven women to the episcopacy in 2016 was one more disruption in the life of The United Methodist Church. Since the solo election of the first woman to the episcopacy in 1980, the largest number of women elected in any of the quadrennial conferences across the globe in one quadrennium had been three, with the exception of 2004–2008, when six women were elected. The total number of persons elected in the class of 2004–2008 was twenty-nine, thus making the women elected in that quadrennium 20 percent of the total. The election of seven women in 2016, however, was another milestone, for those seven were part of a total of only fifteen persons elected that year (46 percent of the total). The demography of the Council of Bishops was being changed. When the Council of Bishops convened for its first meeting of the 2016–2020 quadrennium, there were sixty-four active bishops present, seventeen of whom were women (26 percent).

Sharma D. Lewis

In 2008, Sharma D. Lewis, a pastor in the North Georgia Conference, was elected to that year's jurisdictional conference as a reserve delegate. Four years later, in 2012, North Georgia elected her first in the clergy delegation to the General Conference.

Lewis and many others had anticipated that her colleague and friend, L. Jonathan Holston, would be first elected from the North Georgia Conference in 2012, and then be nominated by the delegation to be its candidate for the episcopacy. "I was shocked," Lewis reported about her election. "You don't usually go from reserve delegate to first-elected in four years!" In the midst of surprise and humility, Lewis received a phone call from a friend as she sat in the session of the conference. "You need to pay attention to what just happened," her friend said, "We need to talk."

Lewis and her friend did meet to talk. It seemed unreal to her that she had been elected before her friend Jonathan. She could not figure out why. "Sharma," said her friend, "North Georgia has been watching you for years. I'm not shocked at what has happened. And I want to ask you to take some time to discern the episcopacy."

Taking time, Lewis sought out those from whom she could receive wise counsel about this new possibility for her ministry. Lewis called Bishop James Swanson, who had been her pastor as a teenager. She consulted with her own bishop, B. Michael Watson, on whose Cabinet she was serving. She talked with her friend, L. Jonathan Holston. At a National Black Clergywomen's meeting in 2008, Lewis had heard Bishop Violet Fisher say that it was time for her to retire. Fisher told Lewis it was time for Lewis to consider becoming a bishop. The National Black Clergywomen lifted Lewis's name as an episcopal candidate in 2012, and voted to support her.

"Now I'm sitting there with being elected number one in the delegation, the affirmation of the National Black Clergywomen, Violet Fisher in my ears, James Swanson in my ear, Mike Watson in my ear. And I said, you know, I need to have God in my ear."

Lewis went away and prayed. Eventually, she concluded she would make herself available as a candidate for election in the 2012 Southeast Jurisdiction.

Without telling anyone of her discernment, she met with the delegation as they considered who they would support for election. As expected, L. Jonathan Holston was selected to be the North Georgia candidate.

But then Lewis really "upset the applecart." She shared with the delegation that, after a long process of prayer and discernment, she was also going to make herself available. "And there was a hush in the room, because here you have the favorite son *and* the unexpected one. I will tell you it was a little tough. There was tension within the delegation. Some thought I needed to wait my turn. What people didn't realize was that I would do nothing to harm Jonathan; we had a great relationship, and his in-laws were some of my biggest supporters in the church I served."

Lewis formed a campaign team as she made herself available as a nominee, but she often felt very alone during the time preceding the jurisdictional conference as well as at the conference itself. Lewis said, "There were some unfortunate things that happened at Lake Junaluska at the jurisdictional conference, including rumors and comments that were defaming of my character." L. Jonathan Holston was elected to the episcopacy in 2012. Sharma D. Lewis was not.

Lewis returned to the North Georgia Conference, but found her soul troubled as she continued to serve as a district superintendent. She says her eyes had been opened to the "dark side" of the candidacy process. She needed to make peace, and she had to forgive some people who had been very mean. She needed to pray and keep discerning, asking God "Are you still calling me to this?" It was an additional four years for Lewis "in a posture of prayer and discernment."

In 2016, Lewis was again elected on the first ballot of the North Georgia Annual Conference, leading the conference's delegation to General Conference. Many anticipated she would be the conference nominee for the episcopacy. Lewis returned to her praying and discernment "because I wanted to make sure. After you go through the election process one time, you don't want to go through the disappointment and hurt of it again." She chose to accept her delegations' support of her as an episcopal candidate in 2016, and was elected by the Southeastern Jurisdictional Conference on the first ballot. She is the first and only African American woman elected from the jurisdiction.

Sue Haupert-Johnson

Sue Haupert-Johnson loved being a pastor in the Florida Annual Conference. She loved life in the local church. She loved planning worship. She loved preaching. She loved every aspect of the work to which she was appointed in the conference. The thought of leaving close relationships was hard: "I also knew I could manage the health of one congregation. I wasn't really wanting to take on the dysfunction of a lot of congregations."

Haupert-Johnson says finding her way into consideration of the episcopacy was like "those old bank-robber movies where the robber is listening to the safe and the tumblers click. I felt like I could mark every time I heard a tumbler click; it was another part of my call. And every time one of those tumblers clicked, I kind of had to pay attention."

As she ministered across the Florida Conference, one group for whom she held a special place in her heart were the local pastors of the conference. At a gathering of pastors from the Florida Keys, Haupert-Johnson found herself in a small group consisting mostly of local pastors. The invitation was for members of the group to pray for and with each other. Haupert-Johnson was not yet a district superintendent or an episcopal candidate when a part-time local pastor in the group began to pray for her. The woman prayed, "God, we know that Sue can be in rooms, conversations, and places that we will never dream of being in. We know we can trust her to represent us and to do well by us. And we know that every room she goes in she has all of us in her heart. Please open more doors for her."

Haupert-Johnson says it was "like God speaking to me." That prayer stirred her to really begin to listen to her call. She knew that the experiences she had, and her life training (including law school), were all part of her preparation to be in larger conversations. She came to understand that her commitment, desire, and calling were to "notice," "listen," "represent," and "speak for an awful lot of folks in churches that need to be spoken for."

The 2016 Southeastern Jurisdiction had elected Sharma Lewis on the first ballot and then, after three men were elected, Sue Haupert-Johnson. As she remembers the jurisdictional conference, she says: "Virtually every person who was there talks about what a tremendous experience of the Holy Spirit there was at that 2016 jurisdictional conference in the Southeast. I think the memory will live forever. We elected five bishops in one day, and the five people who everybody wanted elected were elected. I can't even explain the feeling in the auditorium of just one mind and one heart."

Haupert-Johnson remembers she had prepared many of her friends and colleagues for the difficult and sometimes ugly moments that can transpire in the heat of episcopal election processes. She wanted them to be ready for potential disappointment. In the midst of the natural disasters that had challenged the region, and a national election that seemed to divide people from one another, many continue to reflect that the 2016 Southeastern Jurisdictional Conference was a powerful event where "the power of God was experienced in a tremendous way. It was palpable that the Spirit was at work."

Cynthia Moore-KoiKoi

"This whole process has just been God," insisted Cynthia Moore-KoiKoi, "And one of the things that I have found is that many times women in ministry have those kinds of mystical experiences that affirm what God is doing with their lives and through their ministry. It just seems that God works with us in that way. And I'm so glad that God does!"

Moore-KoiKoi is a fourth generation United Methodist and the daughter of a United Methodist pastor. Her family deliberately made the decision to stay with the strand of Methodism known as United Methodist rather than seeking membership in one of the traditionally black Methodist churches in the US. She says her family "really believes in the strength and power of diversity and working through the messy stuff and getting blessed because of that work. That's part of who I've been."

The journey in The United Methodist Church has not always been easy for her. Within a week of beginning her first appointment to a church in the Baltimore-Washington Conference, a key leader in the congregation made an appointment to visit Moore-KoiKoi in her office. The man was a former chair of the congregation's Staff-Parish Committee and also a leader in the youth program of the church.

They did not have an easy conversation. The man brought to the meeting a comprehensive list of all the reasons women should not be pastors, according to his reading of the Bible. Moore-KoiKoi listened patiently to the man's concerns. When he finished, she said, "Well, you already knew before you came in here that I don't agree with your interpretation of those scriptures. And it really would not be a good use of our time for me to argue that with you. But I am going to make a request that, while I'm appointed here as one of the pastors of this congregation, that you act as if I *am* your pastor. And we'll just see what God does."

Three years later, the announcement came that Moore-KoiKoi was to be reappointed, joining the Baltimore-Washington Conference staff. The man and his wife made another appointment to see Moore-KoiKoi and take her to lunch. Following lunch, they made a request: Would Moore-KoiKoi baptize their (as yet) unborn grandchild? Moore-KoiKoi thanked the couple for their affirmation of her ministry in making such a request and then reminded the couple that such an act would be inappropriate, since she would no longer be one of the pastors of the congregation. As the couple stood to leave the luncheon, the man leaned over and brushed against Moore-KoiKoi's elbow. "There," he said. "I've done it. I've rubbed elbows with a bishop."

"It was a God moment," says Moore-KoiKoi. "Something had happened in our relationship over those three years that enabled him not only to accept a woman as pastor, but also to see and affirm a woman as a potential bishop. That really has been my ministry: to open spaces for folks where God can do transformational work, where folks have labeled people and said because of this label you can't do that."

Moore-KoiKoi, earlier a school psychologist for seventeen years, had numerous occasions when others suggested that they saw her potential as a clergy leader and further projected the possibility she would one day be a bishop of The United Methodist Church. Shortly after her election to be part of the 2016 delegation of the Baltimore-Washington Conference to the General and Jurisdictional Conferences, a mentor and friend of Moore-KoiKoi's, Rev. Joan Carter Rimbach—herself previously considered as a candidate for the episcopacy—revealed that, while Moore-KoiKoi was speaking to the conference, she had heard God say it was Moore-KoiKoi's time to be available.

"Okay," said Moore-KoiKoi to herself, "maybe I need to listen because I really respect Joan. She's been a mentor of mine all along." Moore-KoiKoi called four or five people she knew were gifted in prayer, and asked them to pray for discernment. And she said to her husband, "We need to pray."

Moore-KoiKoi says all those folks did pray with and for her, and they began to come back to her even before she was ready to accept it, saying, "It's been clear in our prayers. You need to make yourself available." Finally, Moore-KoiKoi did hear a direction for her decision-making. She was to offer her name. She did not know if she would be elected, but she chose to be faithful to the prayers and processes, and offered her name as an episcopal candidate.

At the Northeastern Jurisdictional Conference, the balloting began, and decisions about elections were slow in coming. By the tenth ballot with no elections, the conference took a break and Moore-KoiKoi went to Carter Rimbach with a request to convene the delegation for a time of prayer. The delegation gathered and went to the conference's prayer room. A black clergywoman, Helen Fleming, who was not part of the delegation, was also present. A woman with a gift of prayer and prophecy, Fleming was asked to pray. She anointed Moore-KoiKoi and she prayed. "The delegation broke out in tongues." People were praying in tongues, and in the midst of that time, Moore-KoiKoi knew she was going to be elected.

It was a powerful time, but the vision and discernment that took place in the prayer room was not just for Moore-KoiKoi. In the midst of those intense moments of prayer, Moore-KoiKoi also came to know that another African American woman candidate in the Northeast Jurisdiction, LaTrelle Easterling, would also be elected. "I was as certain of it as I was that my name was Cynthia." A short time later, Moore-KoiKoi was elected a bishop of the church, the second African American woman elected in the denomination's 2016 elections.

Tracy Smith Malone

The denomination was not finished, however, with selecting African American women to serve as episcopal leaders in 2016. In the North Central Jurisdiction, another woman, Tracy Smith Malone, was finding herself a strong candidate among those being considered.

Malone is a woman who says she has always given her total, complete life to the church. The daughter of a United Methodist clergy father and an active United Methodist lay mother, her life has been the church. Over the years, there have been many lay and clergy, including her parents, who have counseled Malone that "God has uniquely gifted you and is going to use you one day in extraordinary ways."

Malone says she never imagined what those extraordinary ways would look like, but she tried to live her life with an openness to the Spirit, always asking God, "What is it, Lord? How is it you desire to use me?" Malone lived into every ministry setting to which she was appointed and into every leadership position with a spirit of expectation, trusting and waiting for the "mighty way of how God was going to use me." She did not know the places where God would lead her or the opportunities she would be given to serve, but she was committed to staying open. Her ministry journey has led her to serve in inner-city, suburban, and rural churches, and in African American and cross-racial settings. In most of these, she was the first female or African American. She "witnessed God using [her] in mighty ways."

In 2011, Malone had been appointed a district superintendent in the Northern Illinois Conference. Colleagues and friends began to challenge her, sowing the seed that God was going to use her in a significant way. "We need your leadership beyond just the local church," they said. "There's a broader audience and mission, more people who need to experience your leadership. God's still got something more for you to do." While many were encouraging Malone, a few expressed concern that, even though she had proven leadership and experience at every level of the church, her younger age might be a hindrance to her election.

The 2012 jurisdictional conference for the North Central region came and went. There were no elections to be done at the conference. Many people continued to encourage Malone to consider making herself available for election to the episcopacy. She had been a district superintendent for one year and felt that was the place where God wanted to utilize her at that time. Her husband was a businessman in Chicago, and her daughters were barely teenagers. Further, there was not to be any election in the North Central Jurisdiction that year, although she might have been considered in another jurisdiction.

In 2014, the Northern Illinois Conference determined they would elect delegates to the General Conference two years before the 2016 conference commenced. With the ongoing encouragement of many colleagues, Malone and her husband began to pray. They agreed to "just be open and look for signs." The conference elected her as a delegate to the General Conference on the first ballot. A sign. Arriving at the 2016 General Conference, she was advised that candidates should not make themselves available for chairing a General Conference Committee because they might be vulnerable to criticism that could hinder their candidacy, and yet she was promptly elected to chair the Agenda and Planning Committee. A sign. Her husband and daughters affirmed this calling on her life. A sign. Signs just kept pointing her in the direction of making herself available for broader leadership in the church.

"Okay, Lord," prayed Malone, "Let me fully trust you and let's just see what happens. And so this call to the episcopacy was an evolving process throughout my entire ministry, and it was the call from the community, but finally it was me claiming for myself that it just might be a possibility. And if it were to be so, let it be. I loved serving as a superintendent. I love the local church. I would have been content remaining in Chicago with my family and on the district. But here I am, a bishop. That's my story. I fully claim it. But this journey toward the episcopacy has been evolving over my entire ministry."

Malone was the first of four persons elected in the North Central Jurisdiction in 2016, one of two African American persons elected at that conference. She is the first female elected from the Northern Illinois Conference.

LaTrelle Miller Easterling

Cynthia Moore-KoiKoi had a revelation that two African American women would be elected at the 2016 Northeastern Jurisdictional Conference. In addition to herself, she believed the second woman would be LaTrelle Miller Easterling, a clergywoman from the New England Conference.

Beginning in 2012, and again in 2016, LaTrelle Easterling had been selected as a delegate from the New England Conference to the General and Jurisdictional Conferences. A former lawyer, Easterling was increasingly being encouraged to consider the possibility of election as a bishop.

Easterling determined to spend some time with Bishop Violet Fisher, the first African American woman elected in the Northeastern Jurisdiction. "It was important for me to hear her voice." At a meeting they both attended, Fisher was surprised to see Easterling. As Fisher greeted Easterling, who had hoped to speak with her, Fisher said, "I know why you are here and the answer is yes." Easterling says she had not had any conversation with Fisher about a potential candidacy before.

Other persons, who did not know Easterling well, approached her, and said, "God has spoken to me and said that you need to pursue this." "There was unexpected confirmation from God, from the Spirit, from my family, from people I trust, and then from people I did not even know," said Easterling.

In 2012, Easterling had been elected as a delegate to the General Conference. The tradition of the New England Conference was to lift names of individuals in the conference, not just those first elected, they believed had the gifts and evidence of God's grace to go on to wider service. Easterling's name had been lifted.

When Easterling received a phone call telling her of the delegation's affirmation of her and her ministry and preparation for the work of a bishop, she wept. She wept because she had "no designs on where God would take me. And to hear that my brothers and sisters in the conference believed in my leadership enough, and thought that I had something to contribute on that kind of scale, was amazing to me. That was really the first time that I thought about episcopal service."

Easterling consulted with her bishop, Peter Weaver, about her potential candidacy, and he had counseled her, "LaTrelle, don't inhale. Don't want it so much that if you don't get it you become bitter and broken."

Easterling did not allow her name to go forward from the New England Conference in 2012. She was supporting two other candidates: Aida Irizarry-Fernandez and Martin McLee. She really believed in both of those two persons and wanted to see them elected. McLee was elected.

Again in 2016, Easterling received a phone call saying her name had been lifted by the New England delegation. "Will you consider it?" she was asked. At that point, Easterling says she went into deep prayer and fasting, and had conversations with her husband and their sons. It was something the whole family needed to consider. And then she heard the Holy Spirit say, "It's time."

The Northeastern Jurisdiction has strict rules against "politicking" for the office of bishop. The New England delegation had determined they would support Easterling and a second person. Easterling made it clear to the delegation she did not want any "backdoor politicking." Her request to the delegation was to "never ask another candidate to step aside for my benefit. . . . I saw that happen with Aida Irizarry-Fernandez, and it is a painful thing to observe. I never wanted anyone else to feel the pain I saw reflected in Aida's eyes because of me. This is either God's will or it's not, and I'm fine with that."

From the beginning of the 2016 Northeastern Jurisdictional Conference, Moore-KoiKoi and Easterling had been the two top vote getters. Moore-KoiKoi was elected, and Easterling was one of the first to reach Moore-KoiKoi to celebrate her election.

In the meantime, a third candidate, also from the New England Conference, had emerged and the delegation was concerned. They had selected the two from their conference they wanted to support; the new candidate was not one of those selected. Easterling was aware that ending an evening with one's name at the top of the balloting did not ensure the same the next day. Other persons had in the past ended one day as the highest vote recipient only to awaken and find that serious politicking had occurred during the night to drastically affect the outcome. Easterling says she was "a bundle of emotions, trying to believe whatever happens is going to be God."

The day of Moore-KoiKoi's election ended, and the following morning at 8:55 a.m., a new ballot was taken at the 2016 Northeastern Jurisdictional Conference. The report of the ballot was read at 10:01 a.m., announcing LaTrelle Easterling was elected to the episcopacy, the second African American woman elected that year in the Northeast Jurisdiction, and the fourth African American woman elected across the church in 2016. It was the first time in any election process in one jurisdiction that two African American women (and no others) were elected. "When my name was read, I really was overcome by the notion that I had, in fact, been elected. I still tear up when I think of it. I am humbled beyond belief to serve in this way," says Easterling.

Easterling's only regret is that her mother did not live to see her election. "She was a died-in-the-wool Methodist, remaining with the denomination even through the Central Jurisdiction [a segregated jurisdiction dissolved shortly after the creation of The United Methodist Church in 1968], and even becoming a licensed local pastor after a successful career in banking. She loved the church and would have been overjoyed at the notion that her daughter was serving in this capacity."

It had been sixteen years from the time the first African American woman (Leontine T. C. Kelly) was elected to the episcopacy to the time that three additional African American women were elected in 2000 (Beverly Shamana, Violet Fisher, and Linda Lee). It was another sixteen years until four African American women were elected in 2016 to join the Council of Bishops.

Laurie Haller

"Holy indifference" to the outcome was a theme we often heard from women who made themselves available to be considered for the episcopacy. Laurie Haller was part of the election processes at the North Central Jurisdictional Conference in 2008. She was not elected. In 2012, the number of episcopal areas in the jurisdiction was reduced, there was only one retirement, and the jurisdiction did not hold any elections.

Haller says, "Everything changed from 2008 to 2016 [in the election processes]. In the jurisdiction, you had to have a website, and people were doing all kinds of stuff: traveling to different conferences for interviews, doing Skype interviews, and figuring out how to pay for all of it. It was different for me in 2016 [than in 2008], because I decided that, if I was going to run, I needed to have a *holy indifference* to the process, meaning it wasn't going to matter if I was elected or not. My life would be complete no matter what happened. I was serving in the largest church in the Detroit Annual Conference. I had a great appointment, and I could have easily continued serving there. So, I think that what got me through this process was not wanting it so much. I had to say, 'God, it's okay if this happens, but I'm going to be fine if it doesn't. And I'm not going to be heartbroken again.'"

Haller's journey to the episcopacy began like Sally Dyck's, in the General Conference Mennonite Church, where, following her graduation from Yale Divinity School, she became one of the first women ordained in that denomination. General Conference Mennonites do not have bishops, and do not place priority on liturgy in worship. Haller is a gifted organist and had worked as a director of Music in a United Methodist Church during her training at Yale, giving her some basic knowledge of United Methodism.

While in seminary, she met and married her husband, Gary Haller. Pregnant with their first child when they completed seminary, the Hallers decided to make their home in the West Michigan Conference. During the next eight years, they added two more children to their family, and Laurie served in part-time appointments in the West Michigan Conference, "I had no desire to do anything except help raise our children and serve in a local church."

By 1993, Haller had transferred her membership from the General Conference Mennonite Church into The United Methodist Church. Bishop Donald Ott asked the Hallers to move to Grand Rapids, Michigan, to co-pastor First United Methodist Church. "That's where we cut our teeth in ministry in a big way, at that large church. It was about two years after we started at First Church when one of the office staff persons came to me and said, 'You know, I think some day you might make a good United Methodist bishop. Just think about that, put that in the back of your mind.' I'll never forget that moment, because I had never thought about being a bishop before. . . . I was just trying to put one foot in front of the other."

Haller knew she could never consider episcopal ministry until her children had made their way through the challenges of adolescence and young adulthood: "That's why it's so wonderful that, as women, we need to each be given the opportunity to determine what is best for us. It wasn't ever going to work for me until our children were well launched into their adult lives."

Having sent forth Bishops Matthews and Rader into the episcopacy and having experienced the episcopal leadership of Bishops Craig and Lee, the West Michigan Conference had been continuously open to consideration of women with leadership qualities needed in the episcopacy. Between 1992, when Rader was elected, and 2008, two additional women had been lifted as potential candidates but were not elected.

In 2008, West Michigan Conference supported Haller as their candidate. The jurisdictional conference that year was held in Grand Rapids, Michigan where Haller was appointed as district superintendent: "I'm not a political person. I don't play games. I'm very open and transparent, and what you see is what you get. . . . It was an interesting time for me. I have no regrets about running [in 2008]. I learned a lot about myself and about the church—the good and the bad—but I did not have the support I had hoped for. I was not elected. It was tough to recover from that, because I felt like I was a failure. But I was deeply grateful for the experience and also knew that, whatever happened in the future, I had not compromised my integrity."

2012 passed with no elections taking place in the North Central Jurisdiction. By 2016, Haller was again being considered as a candidate from the West Michigan Conference. There were three others under consideration from the whole Michigan Area (Detroit and West Michigan Conferences). All became candidates and received votes at the North Central Jurisdictional Conference. Haller says, "In 2016 I needed to be clear in my own heart that the decision to run needed to be not only mine, but I needed to hear that from others as well. That was very important to me. I remembered Sharon Rader telling me after the 2008 elections that one of the best ways to be elected a bishop is having gone through the process once before; you learn from the process."

Haller did a lot of soul searching and prayer and fasting. She lived into the *holy indifference* to which she committed herself. She was the fourth person elected in the North Central Jurisdiction in 2016, and joined Tracy Smith Malone as the second woman elected in the jurisdiction that year.

Karen Oliveto

The United Methodist Church was not finished, however, with the election of women bishops in 2016. There would be one more: Karen Oliveto.

At the time of her election, Oliveto was the senior pastor of Glide Memorial United Methodist Church in San Francisco, the fifth largest United Methodist congregation in the United States, with over 12,000 members.

Called into ministry at eleven years of age, Oliveto preached her first sermon at sixteen, and began working as a student pastor when she was eighteen. For nearly thirty-five years, district superintendents and bishops appointed Oliveto to serve in ministry, living a fully authentic life as pastor, academician, and associate dean at the Pacific School of Religion. Oliveto is lesbian and married to Robin Ridenour.

Over the years of her ministry at Glide, Oliveto had been encouraged to consider the episcopacy by those who recognized her gifts and grace for ministry, but she had resisted. By 2015, however she was beginning to think her tenure at Glide was nearing an end, and she had begun to explore other ministry avenues in which to live out her calling. Recruited to consider other ministries both in and beyond the US, Oliveto seemed to be floundering, as she wound up number two in various search processes: "Well God, what are you saying to me? Am I done? Is it time for me to think about retirement?"

The United Methodist General Conference of 2016 began a series of watershed moments for Oliveto, as she recognized that her experience and voice had a place in the larger church of which she had not been aware (or hadn't really owned to that date). The Commission on A Way Forward was established at the General Conference, and Oliveto began to get a sense: "Maybe there's a calling here. Maybe I'm here for this moment." The Commission's task, in part, was to develop a complete examination and possible revision of every paragraph in our *Book of Discipline* regarding human sexuality . . . affirming [the church's] commitment to maintaining and strengthening the unity of the church."[1]

More people began sharing with Oliveto their vision of her as an episcopal leader, and Oliveto kept saying no. Yet she said, "I take seriously that *call* is both what we hear from God and community, and so I began to really pray in earnest, all the while continuing to be really clear. I was not going to run. This had to be a God moment."

A few short weeks after the conclusion of the 2016 General Conference, the California-Nevada Annual Conference was scheduled to convene. With only five days left until the conference would begin, and strongly challenged and encouraged by trusted colleagues to allow her name to come forward for endorsement as a candidate, Oliveto and Ridenour engaged in deep conversation.

Ridenour said she was concerned about Oliveto's prior job searching: "That's not who you are," Oliveto remembers Ridenour saying, "you're called, and you're just trying to fit in."

Oliveto admitted to Ridenour she did not want to harm their relationship. She did not want to harm their beloved church. (Ridenour, a nurse practitioner is a deaconess in The UMC.) Oliveto had a deep fear of what might happen if she became a candidate. They talked about their calls to ministry and Oliveto's fears until Ridenour sat back and said, "You know? Perfect love casts out all fear." Oliveto says that, in that moment, the call crystallized, and they determined they would call their trusted colleagues in the morning to let them know Oliveto would accept the invitation to be available for endorsement by their annual conference.

The following morning, June 12, 2016, Oliveto and Ridenour awoke to the news of the Pulse Nightclub shooting in Orlando, Florida, the worst mass shooting in US history. Rather than fear overtaking them at the violence in that shooting against LGBTQ persons, Oliveto says her overwhelming sense was that "it might be time for another voice at the table. And then it was like the Holy Spirit took over. The annual conference convened, and I prayed 'just let me get out of the way and let God come through.'"

The annual conference endorsed Oliveto as a candidate. In the Western Jurisdictional Conference there were eight others also in consideration. Oliveto's name was number one for all the ballots until her election. "What I loved was we did not run against each other. All nine people. We prayed fiercely together. There was only one election to take place. I just have never walked in the light with a group of people like that. The delegates prayed. I remember the deep prayer, but at some point we stopped, and said, 'We've got to talk.'

"And the conference had a closed meeting. Someone said, 'Here's the question: Talk in small groups about what would happen and how you would feel if we elected an openly LGBT person? What would it mean to you? What would be the impact on your church, on your district, on your conference and on The United Methodist Church?' It was very prayerful. And then someone said, 'What if the most qualified person was LGBT, and we did not elect that person?' That changed the whole tone. And we went back to our voting. There were a couple more ballots and there were only three of us left.

"An ethnic caucus invited the three remaining candidates to sit together to talk about what was going on. Sitting next to the other clergywoman left, who was Latina, I remember looking at her, and I remember just giving it over. I said, 'You know what? She's going to make a fabulous bishop.' And I had this peace. I went upstairs to join the rest of the delegates.

"The next thing I knew the woman was at the microphone withdrawing! 'No,' I thought. 'This is not what God put on my heart.' And then I was elected with all the votes. I've never felt the presence of the Holy Spirit like I did then. And now the Holy Spirit just continues to sustain, to guide, to lead, to lift up."

Karen Oliveto was the seventh woman elected to join the Council of Bishops of The United Methodist Church in the class of 2017. She is the first openly gay or lesbian bishop. She was elected on July 15, 2016.

Note

1. The Commission on A Way Forward Final Report to the Council of Bishops (July 31, 2018), 61, 60.

Part Two

WHAT DIFFERENCE DO WOMEN BISHOPS MAKE?

We began our research with questions. Does having women bishops make a difference? If so, what differences does it make? What does any of this mean for the future? In the election stories were clues to the differences that these bishops may have brought to the church. The election stories reveal insights about discernment of call, reliance on the Holy Spirit, the power of community, the vision of a church that welcomes diverse voices to the table, and the reality of a political process with winners and losers. The elections reveal a denomination that was first to welcome women as leaders at the highest level and that has also welcomed a shift to a far more diverse Council of Bishops. Sadly, the elections also reveal continued resistance to women as leaders in the forms of sexism and racism. Having shared the narratives of how each woman was elected to the episcopacy, we turn, in part 2, to interpretation based on the entirety of our interviews with the living women bishops, both individually and in small groups. A list of the interviews is found in Appendix A.

We asked the bishops to reflect together about the theological understandings that undergird their leadership, the joys and burdens that the episcopacy brought, where they find support, the resistances they encounter, and how they are able to persist. The interviews were wide ranging, and much honest sharing occurred about both the joys and pains they have experienced. The bishops have given the authors permission to search the interviews for insights and descriptions of The United Methodist Church and to share them in this book.

One

EMBODIMENT: BEYOND GOD THE FATHER

The Christian church of Western Europe assumed for many centuries that its leaders should be male. The church reflected the patriarchal cultural values so pervasive for hundreds of years. Reinforcing this practice were the ever-present images of God as father/male and Jesus, the man. The words of the Apostles Creed, "I believe in God, the Father Almighty," were and still are recited Sunday after Sunday in many mainstream Protestant congregations. Stained glass windows emphasize the male disciples and prophets. The Bible contains many images for God, of course, but dominating the images and language describing the Holy has been God as father, God as male, for many centuries.

Karoline M. Lewis wrote in *She*, that when women became leaders in the church, they represented

> . . . a rupture. Being a woman in ministry means that what once was cannot still be. There is a tear in the managerial firmament of the church that cannot be mended, though many will want to try. Women in ministry still represent a disruption in the system, a breaking in of the truth that some do not want to believe: that we, too, are made in the image of God.[1]

117

In order to claim their authority as bishops of The United Methodist Church, these women had to be clear in their own hearts, minds, and spirits that God had called them to this leadership. Bishop Judith Craig affirmed this when she said, "The stories we have to tell are holy stories because we are the embodiment of God's new thing in The United Methodist Church." Finding language to affirm the value of women in God's creation and claim their rightful place in ministry leadership became a major focus for gatherings of clergywomen.

Bishop Susan Morrison remembered, "When we gathered, words burst forth that spoke to us as women. Again and again, those words were so meaningful." Morrison described her experiences in those gatherings:

> My living room became too small. We then met in women-pastor-served facilities. Stories, laughter, and tears were shared. And always we sang. It lifted our spirits so much. The occasional retreat followed. Participants began writing liturgies that used inclusive language and were filled with imagery that spoke to us. Meaningful phrases emerged, and before long Susan Beehler began creating musical settings for them. Others began to add verses and the collaborative music and words wove a tapestry. We lived and sang our faith experiences. It was as if the flood gates had been opened. . . . In those early years, we gathered and sang for survival. The lyrics verbalized how we felt: the isolation, the theologically differing perspectives, the sense of exile in the wilderness.[2]

The music and liturgies created were theologizing—expressing faith that was shaped through experience as women in ministry. Theologizing in the midst of leading the church was both informal, as we see in this Baltimore clergywomen's group, and more formal and scholarly. In the mid-twentieth century, scholars and women appointed as leaders of the church began to reinterpret the biblical passages that had been used to prevent women from being clergy. They did their biblical exegesis and found that the patriarchal passages are not the only point of view present in the Bible. The author of *She*, Karoline Lewis, argues this is the place we must start as we consider women as clergy and as bishops. Women called to ministry and ordination needed to clarify for themselves that the biblical witness would support them.

During the 1960s and 1970s, the first decades when women could be granted full clergy rights in The United Methodist Church, Western culture saw an abundance of dialogue about women and their place in society. In the United States, a movement to include the Equal Rights Amendment in the US Constitution was underway.[3] The work of feminist theologians such as Rosemary Radford Ruether, Sallie McFague, and Mary Daly (see *Beyond God the Father*, published 1973) was gaining traction in the 1970s. They began with the Bible because so much of Christianity claims ultimate authority for the Bible. United Methodists proclaim four sources and guidelines for the theological task: Scripture, tradition, experience, and reason. "Wesley believed that the living core of the Christian faith was revealed in Scripture, illumined by tradition, vivified in personal experience, and confirmed by reason" says the theological section of the current *Book of Discipline*.[4]

Feminist theologians employed these sources and guidelines; they particularly sought to include their own experience as women, which, they argued, had been excluded for centuries by the patriarchal traditions of the church. These scholars combined careful exegetical work with the truths that came from their experiences as women. Literal readings of some texts were challenged by a metaphorical approach. Careful historical study of the cultures from which biblical texts emerged also revealed new interpretations. Jesus was recognized to be one who crossed boundaries and included those who had been excluded, including women. The theological work of feminists was just one of several liberation approaches that became part of Western Christian thought in the twentieth century. Women of color developed Womanist theology that rightfully criticized white women theologians for their lack of attention to white privilege. The dialogue expanded, including more voices from the margins.

These liberation theologies made their way into United Methodist practice. A hymnal was published in 1989, which included newer hymns with a variety of names and images for God. For instance, one hymn referred to God as "womb and birth of time,"[5] a very feminine image. The first line of another hymn reads, "The care the eagle gives her young, safe in her lofty nest, is like the tender love of God."[6] Hymns and liturgies were written and used that broadened the concept of God. The ecumenical Re-Imagining Conference in 1993 experimented with liturgies and symbols that came from the work of the liberation scholars. A sizable minority in the church was excited by the new images and language, which also met stiff resistance. All of this work was connected to the issues around women and their role as leaders of the church.

The feminist and Womanist movements in the wider culture claimed that women's bodies are beautiful and not second class. For those first women who were identified as clergy and then as persons with the gifts and grace required to serve in the episcopacy, embodiment was an ever-present issue. Many of the women bishops we interviewed mentioned that their bodies were constant reminders to others that they are different. They are different because the larger culture continues to expect that bishops are male. Sharon Brown Christopher shared a story about how she came to understand the power of one's body as a symbol:

> I remember a pastors' school when I was a young pastor in Wisconsin. [The leader] was advising pastors about how to go into a new church. And he was saying that the first year you should not tamper with the symbol system of a church. And I stood up and I said, "Lloyd, do you understand that, by showing up, a woman is tampering with the symbol system of a congregation? I don't have a choice about whether I'm going to tamper with the symbol system."

When women became bishops, they could not avoid tampering with the symbol system. Because her very body is a symbol, many of the women bishops said things like, "Some people turned me off before I ever stood up [to preach]." Scholars are continuing to explicate the power that embodiment holds over humans. Nancy Lynne Westfield, religious educator and professor, published *Being Black, Teaching Black* in 2008.[7] This title says it all; our bodies are a message all the time. Women's bodies are not culturally neutral. We bring our body into every room we enter and, with it, arouse assumptions and biases in response. Bishop Matthews addressed this topic while speaking to the Wisconsin Annual Conference in 1981, in an informal setting. She began,

Someone asked me if I were a woman who happens to be a bishop or a bishop who happened to be a woman . . . And my answer, of course, is yes. I am both of those things, though not always at the same time. You waver in your perception of yourself . . . and that's something that I have to constantly be aware of. Every woman clergyperson here is the same way. You constantly weigh what people say to you.[8]

The Wisconsin Conference had been learning from several scholars, including Dr. Rosemary Ruether, about how to find language forms that were inclusive instead of sexist. Both liturgical language and language about human society needed to be broadened. In the above quotation from Bishop Matthews, she used the non-gendered term *clergyperson*, which was just coming into use. Women who would later serve as bishop were watching, learning, and making meaning of the events.

Some used the notion of *wholeness* as they argued for including women in the leadership of the church. With half of the human race excluded, the Council of Bishops and the church could not be whole, they claimed. In 1980, as Matthews became bishop, Sharon Zimmerman Rader was quoted in *The Flyer*, a newsletter of the United Methodist Commission on the Status and Role of Women, "For me as a woman there's a renewed hope—the church has taken a new step toward greater wholeness. Salvation isn't present in the Church until wholeness is."[9] Sharon Brown Christopher stated in the same publication, "Matthews' election is a sign and a symbol. It calls into question all the assumptions about women's inferiority and exposes all those myths we live by."[10]

Matthews herself explained that some had urged the voting delegates to "disregard the fact that you are a woman," but she maintained that being a woman was "an important part of [her] qualification." She would not deny or submerge her identity even though she faced sexist challenges.

There are times when I appreciate being told that I'm cute—though that is not very often. The time I didn't appreciate being told I was cute was at the World Methodist Conference, when I'm all decked out in my robe and my stole, and the big cross that I wear occasionally, and I'm ready for the big parade. Flags, dignitaries, and all the bishops standing in line.

And someone said, "We think you are the cutest little bishop we've ever seen." *Now* that is funny. It wasn't funny at the time. I was taken aback. I thought, I'm wrestling with this constantly, the idea of people thinking I'm playacting being a bishop. I am *not* playacting.[11]

As the first woman bishop, Matthews was prompting these changes in language, understanding, and practice. Rev. Chris Bethke, a Wisconsin Conference clergywoman and friend to Matthews, kept a diary from that time. She describes Matthews as one who cared "about her physical appearance and her self-image." She says that Matthews was very aware of her height and was "determined to turn it around and make it a positive. She tends to use it as a focal point for humor."[12] Bethke observed that she could "laugh about taking advantage of the fact that she looks like a little old lady and how she probably looks helpless."[13] That is only funny when it goes against the expectation of a strong leader.

The bishops' clothing was often jarring to the traditional patriarchal culture. Marjorie Matthews was small of stature. *The Flyer* describes the consecration service in 1980:

> There stood the male bishops robed in black, with their black pants and dark socks and polished black shoes. And there stood Bishop Marjorie Matthews with her black mid-calf length robe exposing nylons and beige, rope wedge sandals. Her stole, designed for the yet unchosen bishops— who were expected to be at least five feet, eight inches tall—dropped from around her neck to the floor and then gently curled up.[14]

She was not an imposing and statuesque figure, but diminutive and gray haired. Matthews was administratively strong and could be tough, but those qualities were accompanied by "a warm, caring, and humanizing demeanor."[15]

Both Susan Morrison and Marjorie Matthews were wearing sandals at the jurisdictional conferences when they were elected. These conferences are held in mid-summer; the weather is often very warm. Without an available change of shoes, they wore sandals (not the usual conservative black shoes) for the consecration service. Bishop Susan Morrison recalls, "I always remember walking down in my sandals because that was all I had. I could hear someone say, 'She's wearing sandals!' People could see toes peeping out from under the robe!" In contrast, Sharon Brown Christopher remembers seeing the men's black shoes below their robes as they shuffled past her kneeling form during her consecration service. Women's bodies *and* their clothing were in contrast to the norm. The norm was challenged again when the candidate for episcopal office was not white. Bishop Linda Lee was advised to straighten her hair and stop wearing African garments if she wanted to be elected.

One of the symbols of the office of bishop has traditionally been the crosier, a staff with a crook on the top. As the bishop is metaphorically the shepherd of her or his flock in the church, the crosier is modeled after the shepherd's staff, with a crook on the top to bring a straying animal back. Ann Sherer's daughter watched her process in to the Missouri Conference with a crosier, and said, "Momma, you look like Little Bo Peep. You've got to do something about this!" No male bishop would make people think of the nursery rhyme character, Little Bo Peep. But the bodies of the women elected bishop matched the character, and the crosier brought it to mind.

As Judith Craig was preparing to go to the jurisdictional conference where she would eventually be elected to the episcopacy, her secretary asked, "What are you going to wear to jurisdictional conference?" Craig answered, "Oh, I've got a couple dresses and suits." Her secretary responded, "Well, that's not enough. You can't wear the same thing twice." Most men at that time probably had a couple of dark blue suits and maybe one black or one brown. White shirts, conservative neckties, and dark dress shoes completed their wardrobes. But women were expected to dress differently. Craig went shopping and bought more clothes. She comments, "You talk about embodiment. She (my secretary) wanted to be sure that I looked good enough." *Looking good enough* was much more complicated for women than for men at that time. Rader was advised, after her non-election in 1988, that one cause was her too colorful, too feminine suits and dresses.

Clothing, hairstyles, weight, and jewelry were all fodder for those people who were critical of these changes. Everything the first women bishops wore and how they looked was inspected and commented on. The range of clothing for men in those decades was much narrower, and the male bishops continued to choose

123

traditional business clothing. Women who wanted to look like women, rather than dress in navy blue suits like the men, were vulnerable!

Stature was also an important aspect of embodiment. Marjorie Matthews was small. In 1979, a second Clergywomen's Consultation began to strategize about electing the first woman bishop for The United Methodist Church. Marjorie Matthews was introduced to the group as a potential candidate. Craig recalled, "Someone shouted, 'Stand up, Marjorie!' 'I *am* standing!' she replied." Perhaps self-deprecating humor along with her small stature contributed to her election as the first woman bishop; she was so small that she did not threaten the male bishops and she could laugh about it. She was not small of intellect, spirit, or competence, of course, but she could be hidden among the taller men in a procession. Several of the next women elected were taller. Bishops Judy Craig and Sharon Brown Christopher were tall. Bishop Leontine Kelly had a large personality and was a powerful preacher in the Black church style. Bishop Elaine Stanovsky remarked, after hearing of how a male clergyperson had tried to "manage" one of her sister bishops, "I'm six feet and one inch tall. That doesn't invite that kind of infantilizing." Embodiment must not be underestimated; it is always present.

Women became the scapegoat for unwanted change. Sharon Brown Christopher shares the story of her work in one area: "I came in to unite two conferences. At that point everything went back to zero, and everybody lost their place in the hierarchical, patriarchal system." Then, because she was the first woman to lead them as a bishop, she embodied the change. The hostility and fear that accompanied the change of structure became focused on the bishop, who happened to be a woman. And her gender was to blame in the eyes of some people.

Judith Craig named this change as *chaos*: "God is doing a new thing. And it's going to be chaotic, just like when Jesus came into Galilee. It was chaotic because he just stirred it up. And we, by our very presence, have started the chaos [by] being such a wonderful community of firsts. By definition, we will be creators of chaos."

In order to justify the rupture of the traditional symbol of bishop as male, many theologians and biblical scholars needed to offer more inclusive understandings of God. Bishop Susan Morrison remembered that, when she was a seminary student, she encountered the theology of Mary Daly and was fascinated with it. She and other women students found these ideas liberating and empowering. Later, Bishop Morrison became the focus of a backlash against feminist theology and the messages released from the Re-Imagining Conference. Morrison remembered, "In many ways I felt, as other women had, that I was translating cultures, even though in many ways I wasn't always accepted in those cultures and understanding that I'm still loved by God." The theological and biblical work that had been done in the twenty years before her election helped to support Morrison's self-image. In the midst of the pain that went along with the resistance to feminist theology and biblical interpretation, Morrison became more convinced of God's grace and the value of diversity.

Bishop Judith Craig, however, needed to reassure the women's caucus at the North Central Jurisdictional Conference that she *was* a feminist before they were ready to support her election: "In the first days of the conference, the women's caucus was not kind to me. They finally called me in, and said, 'We don't think you're a trustworthy feminist' and grilled me." After she satisfied their concerns, the caucus was instrumental in Craig's election. Bishop Craig shared with us that her theology became more progressive during her time as bishop. "The longer I worked with people in that role, the more I understood we needed a wide, wide road to accommodate us. I became less adamant about my theology and more open to other theologies. I came to understand that I don't know it all." However, she added, "The people who stand opposed to my position are children of God as I am." A few minutes later in our interview, Craig led a prayer. She began, "Oh mothering God."

Bishop Rosemarie Wenner's theology begins with the understanding that she is called by God, as all Christians are called, to follow Christ. "It's a recognition from God that I'm valued as a child of God, a daughter of God. And from the very first pages of the Bible, men and women are made in the image of God." She continues, "This is a book written by men, about how they experience God. A lot of encouraging passages [make it clear that] in Christ there is no male or female." Bishop Wenner images God as "a long-caring mother beyond all of us."

The theological work that these women needed to do as they wrestled with their call to ordained ministry, leadership, and the episcopacy appears to have moved most of the earliest bishops to an expansive theology and worldview. Bishop Mary Ann Swenson is grounded in a biblical metaphor of "God setting out a feast in the wilderness" where all are fed, and then they go to feed others. "All means all," she adds. Several of the bishops described being stretched by the episcopacy. Craig said, "My Midwestern simplistic faith got stretched mightily because I found myself in dialog with people who didn't share that view. . . . I shed my childlike ways and became more adult in my theology. . . . It's who the office exposes us to; it's who the office asks us to be in ministry with; who the office asks us to be responsible for and to. It pushes our concepts of God and redemption, evil. All of that." She mused that her theology has continued to evolve since her retirement. "Today, this is what I think Christ means, what I think God is doing. But tomorrow that might not be the same." Bishop Sharon Brown Christopher said that "as a result of the episcopacy, I am learning to be a feather on the breath of God." Morrison said that the episcopacy "broadened me. It deepened my faith. . . . I learned not to judge as much." Sherer said, "I began with a very small tribal God." Now the meaningful theology for her is about "the living Christ, a God and a living Christ who is bigger than even the Christian tradition" amid images of the vastness of the world and the universe. Rader finds her meanings through story, a narrative theology. She recalls that the Evangelical United Brethren tradition of her childhood was more individualistic than her current theology, which focuses on how we learn to live and thrive in a community committed to justice: "If we can't remember that God likes me the way I am, and God likes you the way you are, then I don't know how we even talk to each other." The theology of these bishops appears expansive and inclusive, and they attribute that to the growth that they experienced through the experiences of the office.

Craig believes that the criterion for sound theology is that it "places us in a position of hope for the church." Christopher added, "What the episcopacy and the ordained ministry have done is push me from optimism to hope. And what I mean by that is that I've seen more clearly in the [episcopal] role the underbelly of the beast. And it is not pretty. And yet out of that is how I can hope." Morrison replied, "It didn't slay you." Christopher: "And we haven't slayed it, but we stand in the midst and offer alternatives to [the beast.] The kind of community we have been talking about is an incredible antidote to the beast." These women see the church and world quite clearly with all its complicated realities. They do not lose sight of God's call or shrink from the tasks of leadership, even though the beast is breathing down their necks.

When The United Methodist Church elected women to serve as bishops, it was forced to rethink its theology. If God is only male or father, then women did not seem appropriate for the episcopal office. Revisiting the Bible revealed a plethora of images for God. Some were female. Reading the Bible through feminist and Womanist lenses also revealed Jesus as a man who met those on the margins, including women, with welcome. He made it clear they were part of the kingdom, or reign, of God. Some of this revision of the traditional patriarchal hermeneutic was prompted by what was happening in Western culture. And those women who offered themselves as episcopal candidates came with bodies that reminded constantly they were different. They were embodied. The Church was challenged by the *rupture*. As always in the church, practice and theology interact. Sometimes theology calls for new practices; at other times, practices invite us to reexamine and revise our theologies. The fertile interaction of theology and practice was clearly a part of this rupture.

Notes

1. Karoline M. Lewis, *She: Five Keys to Unlock the Power of Women in Ministry* (Nashville: Abingdon Press, 2016), 167.

2. Susan Morrison continues, "Often the music focused on special moments or concerns. 'A Little Ditty' celebrated the first time there were two women on the Cabinet. 'I'd Take Nothing for the Journey' was a line spoken by an elderly African American woman preacher as she told her story. 'Making Room for the Silences' addressed the need to hear the women on the edges: the racial ethnic, the lesbian, the Third World inhabitant. 'Gather the Cloud of Witnesses' claimed the women pioneers who went before us. 'Zion's Songs' became the community's rallying cry as to what our Call meant. And finally, 'Stepping Out on the Promises' reminded us the future is before us like a joyful benediction." The songbook, *A Shared Journey*, was the result of that collaboration.

3. The amendment's first line is "Section 1. Equality of rights under the law shall not be denied or abridged by the United States or by any state on account of sex." To date it has not been ratified by enough states to become part of the United States Constitution.

4. *The Book of Discipline of The United Methodist Church, 2016* [hereafter the *Discipline*] (Nashville: The United Methodist Publishing House, 2016), ¶105.

5. Brian Wren, "God of Many Names," *The United Methodist Hymnal* (Nashville: United Methodist Publishing House, 1989), 105.

6. R. Deane Postelthwaite, "The Care the Eagle Gives Her Young," *UM Hymnal*, 118.

7. Nancy Lynne Westfield, *Being Black, Teaching Black* (Nashville: Abingdon Press, 2008).

8. Minutes, Wisconsin Annual Conference, June 5, 1981.

9. *The Flyer* (August 31, 1980): 4.

10. *The Flyer*: 4.

11. The Flyer: 4.

12. Chris Bethke Diary, 3. Used by permission.

13. Bethke Diary, 3.

14. *The Flyer*: 4.

15. Jean Caffey Lyles, "An Improbable Episcopal Choice," *Christian Century* (August 1, 1980): 779.

Two

EXPANDING UNDERSTANDINGS
OF THE CHURCH AND THE HOLY SPIRIT

Reform movements in the Judeo-Christian traditions have often involved rethinking what the church is, how it functions, or how it is governed. The ecclesiology of the Methodists was stretched as it began to struggle with the role of women, both lay and clergy, in the nineteenth and twentieth centuries. The Methodist movement had absorbed the patriarchal traditions that came from the Western Christian tradition through the Church of England, and continued through John and Charles Wesley's time. Men governed the church. This practice was connected back to Jesus; the Gospels record his choice of twelve male disciples. Men were called by God to be priests and bishops. In the mid-twentieth century, the growing pressure from both women and men to include women as leaders at the highest level of the church pushed a reexamination of the patriarchal practices. Theology and practice were in dialogue.

John Wesley was willing to allow women to preach in the classes and societies, but he did not appear to question limiting clergy status to men. However, he did break with tradition when he ordained Thomas Coke for the Methodists in the newly independent United States. Wesley was not a bishop; therefore, he was not authorized to ordain. But the Church of England was no longer accepted in the new nation, and ordained clergy were needed to preside at the sacraments.

129

At the Christmas Conference of 1784 in Baltimore, Thomas Coke ordained Francis Asbury, who eventually became the superintendent of the newly formed Methodist Episcopal Church. The ecclesiology that allowed for this break with tradition honored spiritual renewal and sanctification above the mechanics of tradition. The Wesleyan reform movement sought to "reform the nation, particularly the church; and to spread scriptural holiness over the land." In order to keep the movement alive, Wesley realized that he had to ordain.

Such breaks with tradition often rest on an argument for God's grace taking precedence over the rules of the institutional church. We speak of the church being both visible and invisible. The visible church is the institution with its traditions, organization, property, and people. The church invisible is of God. The Preamble to the Constitution of The United Methodist Church states:

> The church is a community of all true believers under the Lordship of Christ. It is the redeemed and redeeming fellowship in which the Word of God is preached by persons divinely called, and the sacraments are duly administered according to Christ's own appointment. Under the discipline of the Holy Spirit the church seeks to provide for the maintenance of worship, the edification of believers, and the redemption of the world.[1]

This definition emphasizes the connection to God through Christ and the Holy Spirit. However, it seems to focus on the members of the church visible, its worship, and the sacraments, Christian education, and mission. In fact, the stated mission of The United Methodist Church is "to make disciples of Jesus Christ for the transformation of the world."[2]

The seeds of ecclesiological understandings that were needed to break with tradition and ordain women have been present in the Methodist movement from the beginning; "under the discipline of the Holy Spirit" leaves room for renewal and transformation. However, it was a long journey and a hard-fought battle that took us from the Christmas Conference in 1784 to the granting of full clergy rights to women in 1956. Once these rights were opened to women, the episcopacy was theoretically open to women too. The phrase, "the sacraments are duly administered according to Christ's own appointment," needed reinterpretation, because the Bible does not show Jesus ordaining women. Yet the church is said to be "under the discipline of the Holy Spirit," the important phrase that allowed for the argument for women's ordination.

Prophetically, Bishop Rader had written in *Images: Women in Transition* (1976), "The developing theology of women promises new life to the intellectual detachment found too often in the church today. Women proclaim hope and a belief in the future as our own basis for remaining in a church so desperately in need of revolution and rebirth."[3]

As we listened to the testimony of the women who have been elected to the episcopacy of The United Methodist Church, their conviction came through loud and clear: their ministry is a response to a call from God. When they are challenged, the conviction that God has called them to serve as bishops sustains them. For the women who are bishops of the church, the Holy Spirit is active, empowering, and clarifying. This conviction is testimony to the ecclesiology or practical theology that undergirds the United Methodist understanding of *church*. As Bishop Steiner Ball said, "[I] understand the episcopacy and election to the episcopacy as a movement of the Spirit, not something that is a political kind of search or a political kind of game." A conversation between Bishops Middleton and Hassinger began with political realities, and then Hassinger said, "Jane, that caused me to have this inner sense of 'I hear what you're saying, but God is telling me something else.'" And Middleton replied, "In all of this, it feels like God has God's way," an affirmation of the activity of the Holy Spirit in the midst of elections. The church is a corporation, with many layers of governance and property worth millions of dollars, but it is also a community actively seeking the guidance of the Holy Spirit. The election of women bishops is a good example of the mix of the institutional and the Holy.

On the surface, we find The United Methodist Church operates much like the government of the United States. It has legislative, executive, and judicial branches and makes its decisions as a representative democracy. We propose and argue, and the majority rules, sometimes leaving a large minority dissatisfied. And yet, a pause for prayer is called before most votes, and a request for the guidance of the Holy Spirit is fervently sought. We follow *Robert's Rules of Order* into complexities of parliamentary procedure when we meet in conference. Our case law is collected and edited every four years into the *Book of Discipline*. When

131

the women bishops share the stories of their elections to the episcopacy, much political strategy is evident. In order to receive enough votes of a jurisdictional conference to be elected (at least 60 percent of those present and voting[4]) a candidate must be well known, have served in appointments that demonstrate spiritual and administrative leadership, be a good communicator, and hold values that match those of the jurisdiction. Also, as one bishop said, "Somebody with power had to put you in the place to qualify."

Yet, underlying these practical (at times conflicted) processes, United Methodist ecclesiology professes a commitment to be guided by the Holy Spirit. The politics of elections are often very visible. Caucus groups and candidates send out mailings to the voting delegates. In some places, delegates receive pieces of paper at the door touting one candidate or another. Candidates vie for visibility that comes from an opportunity to speak to the conference or just be on the platform. In some jurisdictions, they meet with delegations to answer questions and to demonstrate whether they are good candidates for the episcopacy. Bishop Charlene Kammerer remembers being asked about her stance in regard to ordaining homosexual persons at a jurisdictional gathering, telling them that the church might change its mind about that. "I believe that God made us all equal in creation," she said. "I feel called to be open to the possibility [of change in church law]." After this interview, which was publicly reported, forces opposing Kammerer because of her perspective found two other women in the jurisdiction—who held more traditional stances—to support as candidates for bishop. The strategy was to split the vote among now three women candidates. If that strategy had succeeded, none would have been able to be elected. Yet Kammerer became the first woman elected to the episcopacy in the Southeast Jurisdiction. "There were many moments during the first year of my episcopacy that confirmed that I was called to this and by God's grace I was going to do it, was doing it, living it. It was a big rupture in the Southeast, and it was eight more years before the next woman came."

When women were elected to the episcopacy, The United Methodist Church was challenged to a deeper reliance on discernment guided by the Holy Spirit. The inclusion of women in the Council of Bishops required the whole church, guided by the Holy Spirit, to interpret Scripture freshly. Both those who were voting in the elections as well as the candidates themselves had to listen for the guidance of the Holy Spirit to carry them through this *rupture*. Empowered by the Holy Spirit, jurisdictional conference delegates came to see women as equipped and called by God to the episcopacy.

The current dialogue around human sexuality and efforts to ordain and marry persons who are homosexual or transgender has engendered well-organized and highly funded resistance. Both sides of this controversy engage a combination of reason, experience, tradition, and Scripture,[5] coupled with the guidance of the Holy Spirit. That discernment happens under the guidance of the Holy Spirit is not a change for The United Methodist Church. However, the guidance of the Holy Spirit seems particularly urgent in times of transition and change. The *Book of Discipline* says that "our theological task includes the testing, renewal, elaboration, and application of our doctrinal perspective in carrying out our calling 'to spread scriptural holiness over these lands,'"[6] and that our theological task is "creative and critical . . . individual and communal . . . contextual and incarnational . . . essentially practical."[7] United Methodists name Scripture, tradition, experience and reason as the theological sources and criteria for this testing and renewal. Theological convictions are open to fresh interpretation, and our current understanding may not be the best understanding.

Considerable debate and scholarship have been devoted to the relative merits of the four sources: Scripture, tradition, reason and experience. Some have argued that Scripture is supreme. Others argue that Scripture without the corrective interpretation that comes from tradition, reason, and experience is not sufficient. "We open our minds and hearts to the Word of God through the words of human beings inspired by the Holy Spirit" says the *Book of Discipline*.[8] United Methodists welcome the insights that come from biblical scholars in our search for the truth of the biblical message. Scholarship continues, with new insights emerging constantly. The United Methodist practice of including both women and men in the episcopal leadership of the denomination has required the interaction of all four sources as well as listening to hear the guidance of the Holy Spirit. Scripture alone might seem to mitigate against women in leadership roles; many Christian denominations do not yet ordain women or allow them to offer their leadership gifts. Yet careful searching of the Scripture uncovers multiple images for God beside that of male, and offers numerous examples of women used by God as leaders and prophets. Historical study reveals the cultural practices from which biblical texts come. This biblical scholarship and theological reflection have supported the acceptance of women as episcopal leaders.

As women have become part of the highest leadership of The United Methodist Church, they have challenged many historic practices and assumptions. Bishop Jane Middleton reflected, "Any woman, even today, who comes on a path to ordained ministry, is doing a new thing in Christendom. It's still hard. There's still a price to be paid. So, I think for a woman to respond positively to that call, even today, there has to be an inner clarity, an inner strength, a courage that has a deep spiritual basis."

In 1983, Bishop Marjorie Matthews delivered a speech to the World Council of Churches in response to a document on Justice and Human Rights. The question in dispute was whether women could be "worthy" candidates for ordination. She said,

It is my understanding that we believe that those who are baptized into the Christian faith, whether infant or adult, are received into the household of God. We are brothers and sisters, mothers and fathers within the faith, and are expected to share as family members within God's household. Why is it, then, that for many, many years the men of the church have reserved to themselves the joys and trials of service as ordained priests, pastors, or ministers, as though their sisters did not exist? I know the answers that have been given though the ages, but we are living in a day when Christians are being called upon to share our lives in the causes of justice, freedom, and peace for *all* persons—not a chosen few.

There may be persons present who cannot now call me "Sister Bishop." That does not prevent me from calling you my brothers and sisters. I would remind you that in Peter's advice to the early church (I Peter 1 and 2), Christians are advised to grow up! It is my earnest prayer that we *will* grow up as brothers and sisters, truly sharing with each other as members of the household of faith in the houses of God.[9]

134

Bishop Matthews refers to tradition when she speaks of the practice of ordaining only men. She reasons theologically about the meaning of baptism and the concept of the household of God. She refers to Scripture. And experience had shown her that the causes of justice, freedom, and peace must be for all people. Matthews employed all four United Methodist theological resources in one short paragraph! Her argument did not prevail, of course. The World Council of Churches includes many Christian bodies that still do not ordain women.

Until ordination of women became possible in The United Methodist Church in 1956, a woman could not be a bishop. Patriarchal traditions were deeply ingrained in Western Christianity. Challenging them required the use of Scripture, tradition, experience, and reason with the guidance of the Holy Spirit. Models for ordination are found in the Bible. The tradition of setting apart persons with gifts for ministry is well developed in Christendom. As the church struggles to hold its own in a secular culture, leaders must use reason to address new challenges. Experience offers new insights and clarifies questions. Reliance on and presence of the Holy Spirit also becomes heightened in discernment of call to ordained ministry, elections of bishops, and their consecration. "Calls— and the discernment and confirmation of them—are gifts of the Holy Spirit"[10] is part of the opening section on the ministry of the ordained in the *Book of Discipline*. Throughout the process engaged by candidates for ordination as deacons and elders, they are seeking to discern if God is calling them to this, and if they have gifts for ministry.[11] This discernment is partly within the individual, but that call must be confirmed by the community through its own discernment processes at various levels throughout the process. United Methodists expect that the Holy Spirit is an essential part of the discernment for both individual and community. Bishop Joaquina Nhanala said, "I know that I didn't call myself. God called me." And Bishop Debra Wallace-Padgett stated, "If the jurisdiction discerned that I was to be a bishop, then I would interpret that as the community discerning and confirming an inner calling." Bishop Karen Oliveto echoed her: "People started saying, 'We see you having a call for the episcopacy,' and I kept saying no. No. But I take seriously that a call is both from God and community, and so I began to really pray in earnest. And I was really clear. I am not going to run. This has to be a God moment. That's the only way it can be."

For United Methodists engaged in the election of bishops, the Holy Spirit is invoked, expected, and relied upon. Bishop Ann B. Sherer names the reality of this complex process: "What I've come to understand is that many people could be elected to the episcopacy, and some of it is the leading of the Spirit. Some of it is politics. Some of it is resentment and personal self-interest. And some of it is strong idealism and great desire for change and a new day." Marjorie Matthews said, "I've never backed away from an open door that God has put in my way. If God opens that door, I'll go through it."

Bishop Linda Lee claims the Spirit with power. She was elected in 2000, a remarkable year because three African American women were elected. She had been serving on the Cabinet with Bishop Donald Ott. He suggested to her that some people were considering her for bishop. She was not sure and continued to ponder the question. "What I finally prayed to God about was that the only way I'm going to know if this is really Your will or not is if I stay in it. And the vote before I was elected felt like a cosmic shift to me. That's when I knew it was happening. So it was an amazing spiritual time for me."

Bishop Beverly Shamana attested to a deeply spiritual experience in her election.

I felt there was something in the room [where the jurisdictional conference was meeting] that was happening. I had a little statement prepared, but there was something about delivering it that felt like it was not just on paper. I felt a response from the conference that was more than just listening. I felt that they were talking back to me even in silence.

The Holy Spirit speaks both to the individual and through the community. All these are powerful testimonies speaking to the activity of the Holy Spirit in the political activity surrounding episcopal elections.

Bishop Sue Haupert-Johnson was elected in 2016. She described the jurisdictional conference as "a tremendous experience of the Holy Spirit." That conference elected five new bishops "with one mind and one heart. . . . It really was palpable that the Spirit was at work." She is describing the hope of the power of the Spirit come to fruition. Many elections have not been like this one, but even in the midst of a deeply divided church, it happened.

136

The ritual of consecration that concludes the jurisdictional or central conference and marks the entrance of a clergyperson into the episcopacy is a time of heightened awareness of the Holy Spirit for both the new bishop and the gathered congregation. For some, it is a time when the Spirit speaks her confirmation of the elections. Bishop Christopher was elected in 1988. She describes an epiphany as she knelt for her consecration as a bishop: "It was one of those incredible communal experiences of the holy, and movement of Spirit." Bishop Susan Morrison described it in similar terms: "When I was consecrated and experienced the laying on of hands, there was a calm and a sense that I was claimed for this." This sense remained with her as she led the area: "I felt that I was on a journey with the Spirit and with others." Bishop Craig experienced the Spirit at consecration too: "What stands out for me is the moment when you kneel in silence and all the bishops come by. For me that is a period of time that was lifted out of time. It was just holy time."

The United Methodist Church exists as paradox: it is a huge institution with wealth and employees and property to manage. It is also open to "the ongoing creation of a new people by the Holy Spirit."[12] The *Book of Discipline* of 2016 is a book of laws and commitments that spells out in great detail—in 819 pages—the way the church is to operate. Yet we know that the theological reflection undergirding our laws and commitments is always subject to new interpretation through the guidance of the Holy Spirit. That's why we meet again every four years to consider what parts of our laws need to be revised. The people called United Methodist are only human. When they question or struggle with what to do, they most often turn to the concrete laws and procedures that have been established, because waiting for the Holy Spirit to create a new people is unclear and ambiguous. That waiting and listening for the Spirit's guidance is difficult to tolerate, yet it is expected. The United Methodist Church has successfully drawn from the Bible, tradition, and experience, coupled with reason and guidance from the Spirit to come to new understandings of women and their roles as leaders. This theological work is never finished, however. We must persevere in our theological task.

Notes

1. The *Discipline*, p. 25.

2. The *Discipline*, ¶120.

3. Sharon Zimmerman Rader, *Images: Women in Transition*, Janice Grana, ed. (Nashville: The Upper Room, 1976), 8.

4. The *Discipline*, ¶405.2.b.

5. The word *Scripture* is capitalized here, as it is in the *Discipline*.

6. "Section 4—Our Theological Task," the *Discipline*, 2016, ¶105.

7. "The Nature of Our Theological Task," the *Discipline*, ¶105.

8. "Theological Guidelines: Sources and Criteria, Scripture," the *Discipline*, ¶105.

9. Bishop Marjorie Matthews, speech to the World Council of Churches (1983). Copy provided by Rev. Chris Bethke from the Wisconsin Conference archives.

10. The *Discipline*, ¶301.2.

11. The United Methodist Church has two orders of ministry. The elder is ordained to Word, Service, Sacrament, and Order. The deacon is ordained to Word, Service, Compassion and Justice. Both are full clergy but only elders are eligible to be elected as bishops.

12. The *Discipline*, ¶121.

Three

RESISTANCE: SEXISM, TOKENISM, AND CHALLENGE

Within a few centuries after Jesus lived, the Western Christian Church had become a patriarchy with male leadership at the top and male priests wielding considerable power and authority. Women were mostly confined to cloister and habit. Centuries later, Protestant denominations followed that lead. In the Methodist Episcopal Church of the post–Civil War, women fought for the right to serve as deaconesses, an official lay office of the church.[1] Women's rights were front and center at the Methodist Episcopal General Conference in 1888, when the office of deaconess was finally established. The fact that this required debate is an indication of how strong patriarchal values were then.

This resistance was nothing new for Christianity. The deaconess was conceived of in roles that had been reserved for women for many centuries; cloistered women provided important service as nurses and teachers. The Chicago Training School for deaconesses led by Lucy Rider Meyer offered a rigorous curriculum that included Bible, Christian history, and theology along with nursing and teaching. The deaconesses were eager to serve in places of need. Nevertheless, their ministry was primarily confined to being nurses and teachers in urban settings in the late nineteenth century. When they wished to marry, most left their ministry. Laywomen were not voting members of the highest decision-making conferences of the church until that same General Conference of 1888, when five women were elected lay delegates to the Methodist Episcopal General Conference. One of the five was Frances Willard, women's rights activist and head of the Women's Christian Temperance Union. The women were eventually denied participation in the conference. Later, male reserves replaced them.[2] Finally, in 1922, eighteen women were seated as the first female delegates to the General Conference of the Methodist Episcopal Church.

The Women's Society for Christian Service of The Methodist Church, a laywomen's organization, petitioned the General Conference for full clergy rights for women in 1944, 1948, and 1956, but it was not until 1956 that the General Conference of The Methodist Church granted full clergy rights to women. It was a critical step in what had been a long journey from the inclusive early followers of Jesus, through centuries of patriarchy, to anticipating the first woman bishop in Christendom.

The video record of the Uniting Conference, when The Methodist Church and The Evangelical United Brethren Church became The United Methodist Church in 1968, presents a powerful testimony to the lack of diversity in the denomination's leaders.[3] The camera reveals row after row of white men in dark suits and ties sitting at the long narrow conference tables, all facing the stage. Later in the video we see a few African American men, also in suits and ties. The General Conference had approved ordination and full clergy rights for women in 1956, yet women had not broken into the General Conference level of leadership.

Journalist Tom Brokaw has written that "the women's movement of the 1960s came roaring out of the cloistered confines of screened-off examination rooms, suburban kitchens, secretarial pools, and female dormitories."[4] Perhaps Brokaw overstates it, but the late 1960s and 1970s spawned considerable turmoil about the place of women in US culture. The conversation was primarily driven by middle-class white women who wanted more options for their lives beyond keeping house and raising children. And that conversation was occurring in The United Methodist Church too. In 1972, the Women's Division of the newly united denomination pushed for an official study of the role of women in the denomination, and a Study Commission on the Status and Role of Women was formed. (In 1976, the Commission was given full agency status in The United Methodist Church and continues into the present.) Today, the General Commission on the Status and Role of Women (GCSRW) monitors and advocates for the status of both lay- and clergywomen in the denomination, gathering data and statistics as it advocates for full inclusion. Women who were ordained elders in The United Methodist Church began to look more closely at their appointments and to identify a system that kept them in small churches and out of the leadership of the annual conference. In 1964, Bob Dylan sang, "The times, they are a-changin'," but the changes regarding women's leadership in the church were met with resistance and uncertainty at every turn.

When Marjorie Matthews was elected in 1980, the culture of the United States was just opening to the possibility of women as leaders in business, government, sports, and the church. Following the election of bishops in a jurisdiction, the episcopacy committee goes behind closed doors to decide how to assign its bishops to the episcopal areas in their jurisdiction. These assignments are intended to move bishops to new areas every eight years (two quadrennia) and to match the needs of an area with the gifts of a bishop. The North Central Jurisdictional Committee on Episcopacy met late into the night after Matthews' election. The mistaken assumption of those outside the process, according to Craig, was that the committee couldn't find an area that would accept a woman bishop. In fact, Wisconsin had already agreed to receive Matthews as their bishop, and it was placing another that was holding up the committee. Still, Bishop Sharon Rader, who was assigned to Wisconsin after she was elected in 1992, recalled, "Interesting! Because somebody told me years later when I came along, and the question was, 'Can Sharon go to Wisconsin?' There were some people from Wisconsin who said, 'We've had our woman. Let somebody else have one.' So, it wasn't total acceptance on the part of Wisconsin." This story illustrates both the resistance to change and the perception of problems that such change would present.

Leontine Turpeau Current Kelly became the second woman elected bishop in The United Methodist Church, elected just a short time before Judith Craig but in a different jurisdiction. The story of her election illustrates the resistance to women in the episcopacy of some jurisdictions. She had been elected to the General Conference as a clergy delegate by the Virginia Conference in 1980, the first woman from that conference. At the Southeastern Jurisdiction's conference that year she was encouraged to allow her name to be lifted as a candidate for bishop. Her daughter writes, "Veteran power brokers for episcopal elections were shocked; they felt her nomination audacious, as well as ridiculous, and she was not elected." Current describes this phenomenon, "Leontine solicited the support of black church leaders. Many of these leaders were ambivalent toward her candidacy because they feared that her being a black woman would negatively affect the candidacy of the black men aspiring for the episcopacy and reduce their chances."[5] Clearly, some portions of the church continued to assume that white men were normative for the office of bishop. A few token black men were welcomed. But the notion that women or people of color were needed in the leadership of The United Methodist Church was at the bottom of the priority list. Bishop Kelly was elected in 1984, but not by her own jurisdiction.

This description fits the recollections of many of the women elected bishop. Some describe clergymen who were angry, because *they* had "served their time" and believed they were in line for the office. Some had counted on a system that felt orderly and predictable. However, others described men who stepped aside willingly, because they wanted to see the church change. Without the support of male colleagues, the efforts to elect a woman would not have succeeded. The women's caucus simply did not have enough votes, because few women were part of the voting delegations. Kelly was elected in the Western Jurisdiction, which had elected two men who were not white (Bishops Roy Sano and Elias Galvan), and some were reluctant to elect a woman of color as well in 1984! The Western Jurisdiction elected the first Japanese American bishop, the first Hispanic bishop, and the first African American woman bishop. Surely the Holy Spirit was part of the discernment of those delegates.

Bishop Judith Craig says, "Marjorie was elected in 1980, and Tina and I in 1984, and that was the tail end of all the social upheaval of the women's movement. . . . There was just a lot of social stirring. I think when women began to assume the role of episcopacy, there were some in the church who felt that stirring was fresh and new and troublesome." The church was catching up to the changes that were taking place in American culture. Bishop Craig acknowledges,

"We rode the coattails of all that social change. Women, myself included, who were elected were products of the Women's Movement, whether we claimed to be or not."

The times were changing, but the first women had to face many decisions about how to enter into the males-only culture of the Council of Bishops. Judith Craig shares this story:

> When Tina (Kelly) and I were elected, Marjorie (Matthews) was so glad to see us. She was very lonely in the Council. She ate her meals in her hotel room, so I began to eat with her in her hotel room. Finally, I said to her, 'Let's just tell some people we are going to join them for supper.' 'Oh, I can't do that,' she said. It just wasn't her style. [She didn't have the] kind of braggadocio that I carry. She had spent four years by herself [in the Council].

Bishop Susan Morrison, elected in 1988, says, "Even when I was elected, there was still some of the same resistance. You didn't know where to sit because it was very clearly couples. And I, more than once, came in to sit down, and they'd say 'Oh no. We're saving that for so and so.' I found that if I would come in late, then I could sit where I thought I could have a place. That didn't happen all the time, but there was that sense. . . I don't know when we got brave enough to have four or five of us (women) sit at one table."

The sexist resistance in some jurisdictions was particularly protracted. Bishop Charlene Kammerer was the first elected to the clergy portion of the 1996 General Conference delegation from Florida conference. Traditionally, being elected as the first clergy delegate meant that the conference saw that person as a potential bishop. Kammerer said not all those who were happy for her to lead the delegation were willing to think of her as a candidate for bishop. Several other bishops mentioned that persons of color and lay white women were the ones who were quicker to support them as potential bishops.

By 2000, several women had been elected as bishops of The United Methodist Church, but overt resistance continued. Twenty years after Matthews' election, Bishop Ann Sherer was ready for a new episcopal assignment. She had led the Missouri area for twelve years and had hoped her next assignment would be to one of the more southern areas of the South Central Jurisdiction. She reports:

 The year before those assignments were made, the head of the delegation in one of those conferences put out a letter talking about how women and blacks had taken over the leadership of the church. [It was] a very hostile letter, a very frank, sexist, racist letter that said women and blacks are [elected to be bishops] because they're given preferential treatment. They are not the equipped persons. And he concluded, "As long as I'm head of this delegation, I'll be damned if one of them will serve us." And they never did!

As long as that man remained a leader in the jurisdiction, only white men were assigned as bishop to his conference. Those who had been leading the denomination were reluctant to give up their privilege.

The tenacious sexism of the church yet present in the early twenty-first century was illustrated in this story, shared in her election story (p. 102), by Bishop Cynthia Moore-KoiKoi. When she was sent to a new appointment as a pastor, a church member met with her to express his belief that women should not be pastors. He supported his opinion with biblical verses. KoiKoi responded that while she was appointed there, he should act as if she was his pastor. When she left, he acknowledged that she was a good pastor and indicated that he thought she would make a good bishop.

This man's understanding was expanded by knowing a clergywoman, but the resistance to women's leadership continues to this day in some places. One active bishop told us, "I still have clergywomen in my area that are getting death threats." A closed Facebook page for clergywomen who have children at home gives testimony to the resistance that continues unabated in The United Methodist Church. The women face criticism if they bring their children to the church. They face criticism of their parenting. They face criticism when they take maternity leave or need a day off to care for a sick child. Their congregations resist having nursery care available for young children even on Sunday morning, implying that even the pastor should not bring children to their church. Other criticism is more veiled, but still reflects resistance to women clergy. A recent post stated, "I just heard from the SPRC chair at the church I quit pastoring in December that they really like the man who has started serving them. Seems he preaches more like what they were 'used to.' I was there for 3.5 years. Does that mean they never got used to me?"[6] Even today, sexism takes many forms.

Another of the active bishops reported receiving a letter in 2018 that began: "Dear bishop hyphenated name." And she says, "The last sentence was 'you will rot and burn in hell.'" Thirty-seven years after the first woman was elected to the episcopacy, resistance is still vitriolic. Resistance comes from both inside and outside the church. One bishop discovered there are people "who would like to express to me how I am a woman, and I should not be opening my mouth in such matters." Bishop Minerva Carcaño named it as "layers of racism and sexism that pit the community against each other." The resistance that the women bishops encountered sometimes came from other women who were competing for election, sometimes from an argument that she was racially wrong, sometimes from unabashed patriarchal power plays.

One bishop elected in 2016 reported she had received a letter so threatening that it was turned over to the FBI. The angry letter claimed that the area where she had been assigned as bishop "believed in carrying guns and they don't believe in any of the Black Lives Matter stuff. They believe in shooting to kill. And so, it would probably be best if I [did not come.]" Another bishop told us that she seldom speaks anywhere without an armed guard, and must sometimes wear a bullet proof vest.

Bishop Nhanala received a copy of a letter during her first week in office, stating that the writer didn't want a woman as bishop. The letter had been mailed to the president of the central conferences, who forwarded a copy to Nhanala. "I sat with that letter. I said because they don't know that I know, I will keep it as it is. So, I just kept it." The bishop led her Cabinet through a study of the *Book of Discipline*, paying particular attention to the sections affirming women as full participants in the church. Some of her leaders said, "Bishop, you know here we don't have that problem. We are working with you very well." And, she said,

We were working together well. After all that good conversation I told them, you know, I want you to know that I forgave you the very first day

145

when I received what I am about to show you. And there is nothing, just for you to know that I know. So I gave the letter to the secretary to read. And the interesting thing is that one of the pastors said, "Well, you know, Bishop, if the world was being ruled by women we wouldn't have wars." I said, "Well, if it was a man who got that letter, all of us would have been fired."

In 2018, Bishop Nhanala was interviewed about the upcoming episcopal elections in Africa and the challenges she has faced in the office. "As a female pastor, or bishop, not everyone believes you are capable. Some people do not believe in female leadership. It is a challenge to work in such an environment. The general work environment is not bad, but there are still some individuals who do not believe in me," she answered. Yet, when asked if Africa is ready for a second female bishop, she answered, "I strongly believe Africa is ready. The question we should be asking is whether the system of the church is ready to allow more women to enter into episcopacy."[7] The creative women who have risen to the episcopacy in The United Methodist Church have had to confront sexism in all corners of the world.

At the time The UMC was moving toward electing its first women to the episcopacy, American culture was in turmoil and change. Protests against the war in Vietnam had created a deep division. Racism had become a major source of angst and conflict. Bishop Morrison says she sometimes "felt like a child of the sixties in a 1940s job. I felt like I was having to translate into the culture I found myself in."

When the first women were elected bishops, with their feminist convictions and commitments to dismantle patriarchy, the church was settled into a system where men earned their place. Individuals were expected to "move through the chairs" on their way to leadership at higher levels. Yet Bishop Sharma Lewis, who was not elected until 2016 reflected, "There was tension within the delegation that I needed to wait my turn."

Women bishops have relied on the system even as they critique it. Bishop Ann Sherer described how she learned from observing a male bishop: "I quickly realized all I didn't know about what the bishops did. I knew what [Bishop] Ben [Oliphant] did because I'd been on his cabinet. So, I started out doing what Ben did because that's the only model I had even seen, and I'd certainly never seen a woman as bishop." Nearly all of the earliest women elected to the episcopacy had been appointed by a male bishop to conference level leadership positions, which made them visible and prepared them for the role of bishop.

Bishop Sharon Brown Christopher agreed, but added, "Watch out for the undertow. I quickly learned that there was an undertow in every conference. Even though there was a desire for their bishop to succeed, there was always in every place an undertow that wanted to undo and embarrass and to trip me up as a woman." She continued, "Sometimes it showed up in those persons who had been nominees for the episcopacy and lost. And I was told face-to-face, 'You took my place. You robbed me of my place at the table.' There was a hierarchical pecking order, and people worked to get to those spots." Christopher was particularly articulate about the alternative she sought: "The vision I cast was one of community, of inclusiveness, of all people welcome at the table." Several of the women bishops named the undertow as patriarchy.

Tokenism also contributed to the resistance against women as leaders. As she shared the story of her election, one bishop from the North Central Jurisdiction told us, "It looked like I would probably be elected. I remember somebody coming up to me and saying that he thought I ought to drop out. And I said, 'Why?' He said, 'Well, we can't elect *two* women.' I remember actually kind of getting irritated, you know, thinking what difference does it make if we elect two women or two men?" Evidently, he thought that one woman bishop was sufficient, regardless of who might be the best candidate. Bishop Huie's story of her election also illustrates tokenism. After many ballots at the jurisdictional conference, Rhymes Moncure, an African American pastor, withdrew. "Once that happened, people [who had been voting for him] had to decide. I mean, it was really tough for folks. Bless their hearts. I mean, it was really tough for them to think that we were going to have *two* women in the college. You know, the idea that one [Bishop Sherer] was enough. There was a lot of conversation about that. And then in the end, I was elected. It was sort of shocking even to me." The institution had not fully accepted the idea that gender was not a primary qualification for the episcopacy.

The women who were elected in the first twenty years were tested in a variety of ways. Some of it was ideological. Most of the early women were deeply influenced by feminist theology and the values of the feminist movement. Bishop Susan Morrison was attacked after she attended the Re-Imagining Conference in 1993. The conference was an ecumenical gathering of women that pushed the boundaries of feminist theology. A clergywoman member of the conference Morrison was leading at that time had written a book on Sophia [the wisdom of God], which some traditionalists understood as an attack on Christianity and the person of Jesus in particular. Of course, liberation theologies do not attack Christianity; they seek to broaden images of God and to view Jesus in relation to their communities. Morrison said the condemnation of the conference and all who attended "was hell. It just came down like a thunderstorm." Many of the clergywomen who attended the Re-Imagining Conference (and a number of the women bishops who supported them) were loudly disparaged, and their ministry was undermined. Groups who had supported Re-Imagining, like the United Methodist Women, had to defend their existence and withstand efforts to remove their funding. The backlash against feminist theology and women as leaders in the church was strong. Bishop Sharon Brown Christopher analyzes it this way: "That event was used as leverage by the conservative perspectives to derail the women's movement in the life of the church." Sexism resisted the inclusion of women, women's ideas, and feminist theology vociferously.

Another form of sexist resistance showed up as a challenge to the leadership of the woman bishop. An active bishop shared a story of a resolution presented to the annual conference that she believed was an attack on her leadership. She said, "I often wondered if I weren't a female, would [this happen], because I think people look for that vulnerability." Another bishop wondered if her collaborative leadership style invited resistance at times.

Bishop Sharon Rader asked Bishop Nhanala, "Do you think people think that they can tell women they don't know enough because we are newer to leadership in The United Methodist Church?" Bishop Nhanala responded, "I do not need to tell people that I am trained. I know that I am. I do not need to tell them that I have the right to be a bishop. I have the right to be a bishop in this church. I just respond to the argument that is behind it." Rader asked, "So how do you get that assurance?" Nhanala responded, "I know I didn't call myself. God called me."

And Bishop Minerva Carcaño added, "You know the rumor around the church is that [Nhanala] has all women district superintendents. Well, 'shame on her.' So, the way the system bucks and the push back that comes when you take those steps is still so prevalent." Perhaps what made it possible for Bishop Nhanala to bring Mozambique to a place of institutional equity (contrary to rumor, she does *not* have a Cabinet of all women) for men and women was the model of Bishop Ann Sherer, whose Missouri Area conferences had a rich partnership with Mozambique. Bishop Sherer traveled back and forth to Mozambique for many years, and the Africans saw her as a strong woman bishop. Sherer helped them to see that a woman could be an effective episcopal leader. The first women blazed a trail that later ones widened and deepened.

Still much work remains. In another central conference in Africa, at a gathering of women students, Bishop LaTrelle Easterling reported a conversation where women were telling other women not to push so hard for leadership opportunities:

Women in that room were basically telling the other women, "You need to sit down." There is definitely a pall over the women, even in Zimbabwe. Some people pulled me aside, and said "We've got some strong women whose names we would like to put forward for bishop. But we're getting resistance." And in that context, resistance can even be threats. We've come a long way, but there's a long way to go.

Resistance has come from both women and men all around the church. But women globally continue to envision a new church. During the African United Methodist Clergywomen Leadership Development Conference in 2018, the first woman in Mozambique to join the pastoral ministry (in 2004), who later became a District superintendent, Rev. Puleng Maboee, described her longing for more women bishops across Africa: "There is still the challenge of some people thinking clergywomen cannot be good leaders, and they may be discriminated against. More female bishops would get rid of such perceptions," she said.[8]

Even the proper form of address needed attention when women became bishops. Bishop Minerva Carcaño told us,

> When I became bishop, somebody came to me and then another and then another saying, "Oh, we live in different times; we don't need to call you Bishop." And I said, "I'm in a position. It's about respect for the position. [Calling me Bishop] will help remind me that I'm the bishop and have certain responsibility. Please do call me Bishop. You can call me Bishop Minerva, if you want. But call me Bishop."

The office is a sacred trust for the church. It must not be demeaned. Bishops have to resist.

This book tells many stories that illustrate the hold that a patriarchal system had on The United Methodist Church in the 1970s and beyond. The resistance was primarily recognizable as sexism. However, racism and heteronormativity were also unacknowledged predispositions that resisted women as bishops. And allies for women seeking leadership opportunities in The UMC were often persons of color. Bishop Ann B. Sherer, newly elected, found welcome at the Council of Bishops from the central conference bishops. The central conference bishops had only recently been given full voting rights in the Council of Bishops, and many still sat at tables near the back of the room. There were no translators for the Council of Bishops meetings until the Fall 1998 Council meeting; many central conference bishops had difficulty understanding the proceedings. Further, much of the Council's agenda was consumed with concerns of bishops from the United States. Sherer discovered that the central conference bishops were eager to make relationships with her. Those relationships led to deep connections between the Missouri episcopal area and the Mozambique conference.

Patriarchal assumptions were blind to the gifts and evidence of God's grace that persons of color and women would bring to the church. The assumptions that, in order to qualify to be a bishop, one needed to have a certain pedigree, appointments, and offices that provided training and education in the right schools, were probably unconscious in most delegates to the jurisdictional conferences. Yet the clergywomen's caucus, the United Methodist Women, and

GCSRW kept suggesting that perhaps those qualifications could be modified. Bishop Matthews could become the first woman bishop because she exhibited some of those assumed qualities. Her bishop, Dwight Loder, had given her the opportunity to serve as a district superintendent, only the second woman to do so. He recognized that she had gifts and skills for leadership. Serving in that role helped her qualify. She was also a scholar with an earned doctorate. That helped her qualify. Yet she was divorced, and had not put in the years under appointment that most of those who had been elected bishop before her had. Her small stature and gender were marks against her. The clergywomen's caucus was determined to lift her up as a candidate, and to emphasize her qualifications. Somehow, the glass ceiling cracked, and she was elected.

Matthews was a small, white woman who spoke well and claimed authority in a "womanly way." Perhaps that helped as delegates voted for her in 1980. Four years later, when Bishop Craig was being considered for election, some delegates were put off by her expansive gestures and authoritative way of speaking. Bishop Kelly had been divorced and remarried and was African American. She was not endorsed by the Virginia delegation, her home conference. All three of these first women elected were breaking the patriarchal mold because they were women, but in other ways as well.

As Gloria Steinem wrote, "[I]f you've experienced discrimination in one form, you're more likely to recognize it in another. Also, racism and sexism are intertwined—and cannot be uprooted separately."[9] The clergywomen's caucus and other groups advocating for the inclusion of women also supported election of persons of color and other minorities. These groups worked together to break the hold patriarchy and racism had on the institution. Eventually, the church agreed to ensure that all of its committees included young and old, men and women, laity and clergy, and a variety of ethnicities and races from all jurisdictions. The pattern of election, however, continued to demonstrate racism and sexism. Sixteen years intervened between elections of African American women to the episcopacy. Kelly was elected in 1984. Finally, in 2000, three additional African American women were elected: Beverly J. Shamana, Violet L. Fisher, and Linda Lee. And again, it was another sixteen years for Cynthia Moore-KoiKoi, Tracy Smith Malone, and LaTrelle Easterling to join the Council

151

of Bishops. In the stories of their elections, many bishops recount being told that if the jurisdiction elected an African American man, there would not be support for a woman of color. The assumption continued that the norm for election to the episcopacy is white, European American, male, and that one token "other" was enough.

With the addition to the *Book of Discipline* in 1972, of language condemning the practice of homosexuality as "incompatible with Christian teaching,"[10] the stakes became higher for any candidate who was not heterosexual. The unwritten rules of patriarchy favored men who were high achievers and were married with children. Anyone, male or female, who did not fit that mold needed to be very private about their personal life. The first *openly* gay or lesbian bishop was elected in 2016. Bishop Karen Oliveto was very public and affirming about her wife, Deaconess Robin Ridenour, and the Western Jurisdiction elected Oliveto unanimously and hoped to guide The United Methodist Church from this movement in their jurisdiction. Charges and court cases to the contrary, Oliveto continues to serve the Mountain Sky Episcopal Area with high approval.

As Jeanne Audrey Powers had predicted, women were elected to the episcopacy in The United Methodist Church. Sexist ideas, racism, and homophobic institutional practices were challenged. Conflict and tension were the result. Yet God continued to call diverse women to this office. Bishop Debra Wallace-Padgett told us, "If the jurisdiction elected me as a bishop, then I would interpret that as the church community confirming that God had called me to the episcopacy." Women discern a call to the episcopacy both individually and through the community. Delegates to jurisdictional conferences continue to discern that call in both women and men as they cast their ballots. By 2016, thirty-four women had been elected to the episcopacy in The United Methodist Church.

Notes

1. In the Methodist Protestant Church, however, women were ordained as early as 1866, with full clergy orders granted to women in the 1870s. When they merged with the Methodist Episcopal Church and the Methodist Episcopal Church-South in 1939, they had to eliminate women's ordinations.

2. See "Timeline of Women in Methodism," http://www.umc.org/who-we-are/timeline-of-women-in-methodism, accessed November 2, 2017.

3. http://www.umc.org/who-we-are/methodist-history-the-uniting-conference-of-1968, accessed October 26, 2018.

4. Tom Brokaw, *Boom! Talking about the Sixties* (New York: Random House, 2007), 202.

5. Angela Current, *Breaking Barriers: An African American Family and the Methodist Story* (Nashville: Abingdon Press, 2001), 106.

6. Margaret Ann Crain is a member of this closed Facebook group. She quotes this but honors the confidentiality of the individual who posted it.

7. Eveline Chikwanah, "Nhanala: 'Africa is ready' for second female bishop," United Methodist News Service (August 17, 2018, Mutare, Zimbabwe), https://www.umnews.org/en/news/nhanala-africa-is-ready-for-second-female-bishop, accessed September 17, 2018.

8. Eveline Chikwanah, "African clergywomen making great strides," United Methodist News Service, Mutare, Zimbabwe, https://www.umnews.org/en/news/africa-clergywomen-making-great-strides, accessed August 10, 2018.

9. Gloria Steinem, *My Life on the Road* (New York: Random House, 2016), 49.

10. The Social Principles, the *Discipline*, ¶161.G.

Four

BEING A CHANGE AGENT
AND CLAIMING AUTHORITY

In 2017, Bishop Judith Craig reflected on the advent of women in the office of bishop and what difference it made:

I think what we offered was a different style of leadership. It is hard to put your finger on it. We simply came at things more collegially. I think we softened authority, made it more acceptable because we were a softer people. We approached things differently. And so, bit by bit, the possibilities of seeing leaders differently and leaders leading differently has trickled out. I don't want to say trickled down. It trickled out. We have modeled a different way. I think it needs to be contagious in the life of the church. It has certainly been contagious in the life of the Council of Bishops. And there are enough of us now that a lot of the church has experienced a woman's leadership. Not all women leaders are exactly the same. I don't mean to say that. But I do think women in general come at things more collegially; just by nature we are more attentive to the side issues. I just think that is the natural way women are.

"Enough of us now," said Craig. Indeed, the notion of a critical mass is relevant as we consider the difference that women have made in The United Methodist Church. Jay Newton-Small, writing in *Time Magazine*, said, "[W]hen women comprise 20% to 30% of an institution, things begin to change."[1] In 2018, of the one-hundred-sixty-four total members of the Council of Bishops, thirty-two were women or 19.5 percent; sixteen women were active bishops out of a total of sixty-six (24 percent). The critical mass is at hand.

So, if there is a critical mass of women in episcopal leadership, what kind of leadership are they offering? Bishop Craig was elected as a bishop in 1984. She has had many years to observe the effects of her sister bishops on the church and to think about leadership. She believes that women have brought the attribute of *softness*. "*Softness* is not a chicken word. Real softness is tough because softness cares about what's going on and doesn't want to hurt people. But at the same time, it can be very tough and straightforward." She continued to name attributes for leaders: a sense of assurance, willingness to be authoritative when you must, sensitivity to other people, and a commitment to continually study the culture and the theology in which you are working. "What is God doing here? What does God want here? Every year, God wants something new. God never settles down, so we can't ever settle down," Craig says.

But at the time of her election, issues of sexism and gender were raised. *The Flyer*, a newsletter published by the General Commission on the Status and Role of Women, contains a story by Patricia Broughton about Craig's election. She observed, "Women questioned her feminist commitment and men her non-traditional demeanor."[2] Jeanne Audrey Powers is quoted in the same issue: "She's comfortable with the authority she has and will give others room to maneuver." Craig had arrived at the jurisdictional conference at peace with her decision to allow her name to be in the mix. Broughton wrote, "It was that peace—and the confidence that radiated from it—that both hindered and aided Craig in her episcopal quest. From the outset came questions about her style, her large, confident gestures, her 'aggressive, take-charge manner.' "[3] This is the dilemma that many women face; confidence and willingness to take authority is needed, but too much is seen as unwomanly. Craig's analysis in 1984 was, "Confidence is harder to take in a woman."[4] Nearly forty years later, this continues to be an issue for some leaders who are women.

Not all women or men lead in the same way; stereotypes linking gender and leadership style simply do not hold up in reality. Some women bishops are quite authoritative, and some male bishops are collegial. Bishop Susan Morrison describes her leadership as collegial and empathetic: "I like building community . . . I listen well. I'm extremely intuitive. I can usually tell by a gesture when someone's upset."[5] The question one might ask is, how did she know how to lead in that way? The earliest women in the episcopal office had only men as models for how to claim the authority of the office appropriately. While there were men who sought to lead in a collegial fashion, the predominant model had been of a leader who was "in charge," a decision maker, a person who spoke and everyone listened and obeyed. Rader remembered an early meeting with the Cabinet (district superintendents) in Wisconsin when one superintendent reflected about the change the group was experiencing. "Do you understand you are asking us to operate in a very different way than we have been trained by your predecessor?" he asked.

Bishop Linda Lee said, "The office grows us,"[6] which seems to suggest that she learned about what leadership was needed while in office. No single method of leadership is adequate in the role of bishop. The same person may lead in a variety of ways depending on the situation. Bishop Susan Hassinger reflected on the shifts in leadership style that she had employed over the years:

> I came into episcopacy from being eight years on conference staff, in a consulting role. I started out like a consultant and that only works so far, because there comes a time when you have to make the decision. So that was one shift. Then I began to realize I needed to be a teacher, in a teaching role. I was going out in various ways to do that. After doing a thirty-day spiritual exercise, my key role was as spiritual guide, not administrative. Then, when I got into the retirement community, working with my two annual conferences as an interim, plus three other annual conferences, my role was as a midwife, where my job was to help the birthing pangs, the birthing pains, the contractions that happen. I needed to be with people as they did this, help them to breathe, and then I could walk away, and they had to take care of the baby.

Perhaps one characteristic that allowed Bishop Craig to serve successfully for sixteen years was her sense of humor. Bishop Craig readily displayed the ability to laugh at herself, as did several of the earliest bishops. When asked for advice to women who are leaders in the church, she replied, "Don't take yourself too seriously. I think a lot of my comfort and ability to do what I did had to do with my sense of humor and the fact that I don't take myself too seriously." Bishop Matthews' self-deprecating humor was welcome respite from the serious consideration of women as episcopal leaders. Bishop Susan Morrison displayed this quality too. Here is a story she shared:

> Bays Chapel in Eastern Pennsylvania is one of the old, classic churches . . . historical churches, Evangelical tradition. And they remodeled it, and so I came for the dedication; it was a big deal. And it was just one room with a balcony over it, like the old church would be. Of course, the pulpit is right in the center, and you go up these steps to it. And they had planned to have a circuit rider, with a horse. After the service, you know, I was going to send him off over the hills. It was in the countryside. So, the service began, and it was processional time, and I'm at the end of it. And we came in on "O For a Thousand Tongues to Sing." We got to about the sixth verse, and I got to my place up front on the side. As we're singing the last verse of the hymn, I feel a plop in the top of my head. And I reach up, and the person behind me grabs my arm and says, "Bishop, don't move. It's a wad of bubble gum." But it was too late. I had already touched it, which meant it had gotten into my hair. So, someone ran to the organist and said, keep playing. So they went back. No one knew the verses. They whispered around to say, does someone have a knife or scissors, so we can cut the bubblegum out of the bishop's hair? So finally, that happened, and I preached, and I felt like Friar Tuck. And the service was over, and we process out. We all gather around the horse with its circuit rider. I'm supposed to raise my hand and give the benediction. Circuit rider is to climb on the horse and take off over the hill. And as I . . . honest to God, this is the truth . . . as I raise my hand to give the benediction, the horse loudly passed gas. I lost it. The whole place lost it.

Bishop Morrison clearly enjoyed the joke. Yet she also affirmed that she saw the great "level of respect that was for the person who was in the office. It wasn't you. And so, you handled it more tenderly or caringly, knowing the level of respect that came with it."

Morrison and Craig both claimed that their sense of humor was expressed in a willingness to play. They made time to play with their Cabinets and other leaders. Morrison recalled attending Georgetown basketball games with the Cabinet. "We had a good time," she said with a smile. Craig responded, "I was a party kid. I like parties with my staff and crazy things like, if you wear a tie to my house, I'll cut it off. And I really did." Her memory illustrates that most of the leadership and staff were men.

Along with their willingness to laugh, those first few who were elected felt a special responsibility to be *very* good bishops. "I was very aware and Tina [Bishop Leontine Kelly] was too, that we had better not botch it. . . . I was aware that I was being watched, and what I did would reflect on a future generation." Craig was surprised that those who watched carefully also listened. "I kept saying the things I had said before, but now people wrote them down! People really hung on my words." With authority comes the need to be careful what you say.

In order to claim their authority as bishops of the church, these women had to be clear in their own hearts, minds, and spirits that God had called them to this leadership. And they sought to claim it in their own ways. Several of the active bishops called it *authenticity*. Bishop LaTrelle Easterling, elected in 2016, told us that "authenticity brings holy boldness." This authentic boldness was evident in several of the stories of election that the bishops shared with us. Bishop Charlene Kammerer experienced this scrutiny when she was being interviewed by delegates to the jurisdictional conference that would ultimately elect her. Her answer—"I would support the position of the church in regard to human sexuality, but that I was open to the possibility that we as a church could change our mind at some point in the future"—was "like throwing a nuclear bomb in that room." She knew that this answer was not what many wanted to hear, and yet she needed to speak her truth. Bishop Sally Dyck asserted that, "No matter what you say, somebody's going to turn it against you. And (sometimes) they're ugly about it." She sought to remain authentic in spite of the political price she might pay. Bishop Janice Huie shared a similar story. Prior to her election, she was meeting with the jurisdictional delegation from a particular conference and was asked about Promise Keepers, a conservative men's group that was politically powerful at that time. "I don't know what came over me to say this. But I just looked at them and said, 'I wouldn't have any idea. They don't let me come.' And I sat down. There was just this little moment inside me that I'd had enough!" That answer could have been political suicide, but it was authentic and honest. Authenticity is another way of describing what the author of *She* called "leading from the soul."[7] These women clearly attended to this value.

As Bishop Craig said, the women who have been elected are quite diverse. Not only do they lead differently, they also come with a variety of particular skills and interests. Bishop Beverly Shamana is an artist and a musician. She called on those gifts as she led her annual conference, her Cabinet, and in the Council of Bishops. Bishop Linda Lee has a particular gift of spiritual formation and spiritual direction. Her time in the Wisconsin area brought attention to the spiritual lives and practices of her people. Every bishop has gifts for administration, leadership, and preaching, of course, but these women used their other gifts as starting points for much of their leadership. For the church to see that these gifts might be used to lead an annual conference was a stretch in some cases. Shamana said, "I am hoping that some women will feel free to use whatever gifts they have honed or own or have been given to them by God, [and] find a way to be true to themselves and not simply put that aside and think that's not appropriate for the episcopacy." Each bishop is a unique woman and brings her gifts and knowledge to the leadership role.

Being authentic is part of the difference that women are making in the episcopacy. Bishop Laurie Haller is the first woman bishop in Iowa, and authenticity is a high value for her. "I am not going to pretend to be somebody that I'm not. I don't want any of our clergy to feel that they have to be someone that they're not [in order to] be successful in their ministries." Bishop Deborah Kiesey echoed this when she said, "Intentionally being myself in the role is to be open and accessible to people and not to build a wall." She had realized that her leadership style was not what people expected. "When I was growing up, I thought in order to be a bishop you had to be tall and gray-haired and a man," but now she is comfortable with herself in the role. Bishop Easterling commented, "In our college, they keep telling Cynthia [Moore-KoiKoi] and me that they feel a newness, a freshness, because we are there. I think we are just being who we are." Part of who they are is women who claim their voices.

Bishop Jane Middleton mused, "From our first days as pastors, we had to claim an inner authority, because it was not given to us." The first women who served as bishops were clearly relying on an inner authority. Bishop Matthews said that she had no role model to follow, since she was the first. Yet, if God opened that door, she would walk through it.[8] The confidence to become the first clearly came from an inner authority and clarity of call.

More than thirty years later, Bishop Dyck observed that many of her male colleagues and friends appear to be "so incredibly confident of their ability to know what exactly needs to happen." She, however, thinks, "I'm not really sure I do have a total read on this, or a total idea as to what we need to do. I need more heads to think this through. And that will clarify what I need to do as a bishop. That is my analysis of collaboration." She attributes this leadership style difference to socialization. "In these times of adaptive challenges, I think it works for us. It comes more naturally to us [women]." Perhaps this also comes from her Mennonite roots, a quiet but strong and steady leadership style that includes listening. Bishop Dyck, along with Bishops Oliveto and Middleton, were named by their sister bishops in 2017 as ones who had been particularly courageous leaders. They "have led in an incredible, risk-taking way and help us to trust being open and guided by the Holy Spirit."

Bishop Fierro Harvey remembers asking her Cabinet, "Are we all willing to hold hands and jump off together? Because if not, I'm *not* going by myself." She waits until the leaders can reach consensus. "Unless we can all agree, and sometimes agree to disagree, we're not walking out of the door." She has also tried to limit the voting of the annual conference, where the body debates, and then a vote is taken with the majority ruling. Instead, they work toward consensus.

Bishop Rader observes that the women who had been some of the first to be ordained were seen as a risk for the church. She heard in the stories of the women bishops that they too had lived in the risk. "The safe places aren't always where you're supposed to be," she said. Bishop Jane Middleton said, "I didn't even know a woman could do this, to be a pastor, let alone be a leader, let alone be a bishop."

Some of the more concrete evidence of the change that women bishops brought to the church was seen in their offices and in how meeting spaces were organized. Bishop Sharon Rader is famous for changing to round tables at meetings of the Council of Bishops. Craig called that change "significant in the life of the Council." Morrison remembered that the women bishops were "usually in the back of the room because in those days there was a hierarchy of where you sat at the table, to say nothing about whether you spoke or not." In 1996, Rader had been elected as secretary of the Council of Bishops. She remembered:

They (the Council) were always talking about how we needed to talk to each other more, and there were questions about where the general secretaries ought to sit. The plenary sessions were set up with tables in the back of the room for general secretaries, visitors, and press. The rest of us were sitting in two or three rows in an open U, looking at the back of the head of the person in front of us. It was very formal, and we all wore suits and dressed up and looked very nice. It was a long time ago. So, I wondered with the Executive Committee what would happen if we sat at round tables where we could look at each other and talk more easily to each other. And the Executive Committee said, "Well, we'll try it once." And I said, "Fine." It was a big deal to get round tables, particularly at Junaluska. They weren't prepared for us to do it. We've never gone back to those straight tables and rows.

Bishop Sharon Brown Christopher added, "Oh, I think the round table pushed the whole Council, men and women, to form relationships with one another in ways that relationships had not been formed before. So, it became a much more relational body, because we sat together and talked."

Other bishops shared stories of how they changed their offices to fit themselves and their understanding of leadership. Bishop Janice Huie, who is not very tall, was assigned to Arkansas and followed Bishop Wilke, who was quite tall. "So I walk in, and I go sit down behind the desk in the biggest office chair I have ever seen in my life. My feet couldn't touch the floor, and if I leaned back the chair was going to tip over. And I sat there for the longest time thinking, 'Oh my goodness! I knew this was a really big job, but . . . God help me to do it. But not in this chair!'" She described this as a decisive, symbolic moment, where she realized that she needed to be bishop in a way that "fit" or was authentic for her. Bishop Charlene Kammerer wanted to open the curtains to her office and see the world, both figuratively and concretely. Bishops Hassinger and Kiesey chimed in, describing office furniture they had added that included small tables where conversations could happen without the barrier of a large desk in between. "I went in, and it was a big heavy desk. It said, "I'm in charge." But I can't separate myself from people like that."

The conversation then turned to how the unwritten rules of the Council of Bishops began to change when women were elected. Bishop Easterling told us, "When I began to inquire about when the shift had happened, it always pointed back to women bishops who had said, 'This is not the best way to do this.'" Even in 2018, the Council of Bishops struggles to find a way to lead the denomination. Bishop Bruce Ough, speaking to the Council when it met in April 2018, said, "We are a large Council, we meet infrequently; we are elected regionally and generally feel more affinity and loyalty to our residential and regional constituencies than we do to the whole church. . . . We are not a leadership group for the church . . . we are simply a group of leaders."[9] Perhaps this description helps to explain why, when women became part of the Council expecting community and collegiality, they struggled to find their way. In that setting, the women bishops sought to create more dialogue and less hierarchy. Rader commented, "Tina [Kelly] came in 1984 and heard that the norm is that your first quadrennium you sit and be quiet. And she said, 'I've got four years here, and if I wait for the next quadrennium I'm done.'" Craig added, "I think she kind of broke that pattern and that tradition because she popped up very early in the quadrennium. But boy, if she had something to say, it was worth listening to." Bishop Ann Sherer observed that the bishops from central conferences were not voting members of the Council of Bishops until 1988. When she became a bishop in 1992, she found the central conference bishops eager to quickly form close relationships with the newly elected women. "They welcomed us into the community and were eager for relationships. In some ways, we were two groups of outsiders." The culture of the Council was changing, but slowly.

An unwritten rule of the Council of Bishops culture required that all conflict in the Council be kept private. Bishops were "supposed to *handle it*" if it would embarrass the Council. So, when fifteen bishops, five of them women [Kelly, Craig, Morrison, Rader, Swenson], signed on to a document in 1996, urging the church to cease its condemnation of homosexuality, the rule was shattered. The document did not represent the whole Council, and it had not been shared with the Council before it was released to the public. It was received with great joy by some and with terrible disapproval by others. The Denver 15 broke the rule that all bishops were to speak with one voice. Bishop Craig is proud of her role in that action: "I believe we put a lever under the rock and let the snakes fall out." She admits that the signers may have made a "mistake in methodology." Bishop Mary Ann Swenson experienced the action as freeing for her: "Even when the other bishops were coming down on us day after day in our meetings," Swenson felt freed because everyone knew where she stood on that issue.

Several bishops shared stories of how they were shunned after that action, as well as how some people supported them even when they did not agree. That was clearly a time of intense feelings all around the church and especially among the bishops on all sides. Craig called the response of the Council a "tongue lashing." Swenson said, "It was hard not understanding the rules of the culture in the Council of Bishops. It didn't dawn on me that we had broken some major covenant." The five women included Kelly, who was retired; the other four were active bishops at that time. All five suffered as a consequence, as did the men who were signers. In spite of the negative response from the Council, perhaps the action had some effect in freeing bishops of the church to speak their conscience on a variety of matters. Those who authored the Denver 15 statement made authenticity a higher value than protecting the monolithic voice of the Council.

The United Methodist Church was working hard in the 1980s and after to clarify its policies around sexual ethics as well as its response to sexual misconduct cases. Through the work of a variety of leaders, the General Commission on the Status and Role of Women (GCSRW) took the lead in training and raising consciousness. Anita Wood recalls working with Naomi Southard to write a sexual ethics policy to send to General Conference in 1988. After Cecelia Long became part of the General Secretariat of GCSRW in 1989, she and Stephanie

Hixon began writing training material for bishops and Cabinets on issues of sexual abuse and sexual harassment. They advocated for training of all bishops and clergy on a regular basis and offered the initial training events. Soon, their attention, along with leaders from the Women's Division, the General Board of Church and Society, and the General Board of Higher Education and Ministry, turned to the laity of the church. "We were all very concerned that the clergy were being trained on some issues, but there was little to nothing being done to help the lay people understand and grapple with the issue."[10]

In the Council of Bishops, women helped one another to learn how to deal with charges of sexual misconduct. Bishop Craig even organized a role play for newer women bishops to practice clear communication with the perpetrator. Most of the women bishops we interviewed mentioned that they had received numerous complaints about sexual misconduct. "It's almost like Momma's in the house, and now we can talk, and you will hear us," mused Bishop Sharma Lewis. Having a woman bishop at the highest level in an annual conference may have emboldened victims to come forward. Like the #MeToo movement of 2017–2018, once one case had been heard and the perpetrator had been removed from ministry, other victims would speak up. Bishop Lewis's analysis is, "Having a woman there, they feel more of a freedom to be able to talk to us about important things, knowing that we will listen. We will not judge, but we will act when we need to and not just ignore issues. . . . When women are in the house, there's a different feel about how much we need to share about the machismo stuff that hurts." Bishop Peggy Johnson was told by a woman making a charge, "I know you will hear me." This may be one of the most significant differences that female bishops have prompted in the church. Sexual ethics charges have been heard and acted upon. Institutions headed only by men have, perhaps, been slower to respond.

The North Central Jurisdiction College of Bishops was particularly aware because of a situation in the Evangelical Lutheran Church of America in Wisconsin, where a male bishop had been charged and removed. When Craig was assigned to West Ohio in 1992, she had already been bishop in Michigan for eight years. The female assistant to the Lutheran bishop had been invited by Bishop Craig to West Michigan to assist in developing sexual ethics policies and to conduct trainings for clergy. The goal was to make clear what behaviors were chargeable offenses.

Craig was convinced that the victims of sexual misconduct should be heard, but also needed to be cared for. She set up networks of support. In West Ohio, Reverend Anita Wood recalls being asked by Craig if she would be willing to talk to people bringing complaints, not to talk them out of the complaint, but to offer a listening ear and support. Wood was serving on the Commission on the Status and Role of Women at the time. Looking back, Wood believes that Craig's two-pronged approach made a real difference for the conference. Perpetrators were held responsible and removed from ministry. Victims were heard and supported.

This work was very stressful. As the interview group of early bishops talked, Rader reminded Craig, "You were one of the first to get a conference policy." Bishop Craig remembered, "The first couple times I did interventions with sexual misconduct, I shook a little. When I asked for a pastor's credentials, I was asking for his life." Following one of those sexual ethics training meetings, Craig said:

> One pastor came up to me and said, "I'm the man." And he was a leading conservative pastor, big church. And I was supposed to preach in his church Sunday morning. So he handed me his credentials on Saturday. . . . And I went in there and preached on Sunday.

Craig recalls that she was "shaking in her boots," but she did what needed to be done. Those were the years when sexual misconduct became a major issue. As Craig remembers,

> People were coming out of the woodwork. We were, I think all of us, dealing with lots of cases, more than our predecessors ever did. I don't know if there's a correlation [between the first women bishops and charges being filed by victims of sexual abuse] or not. In my eight years, I dealt with sixty-four and never had a trial.

She never had a trial, because the situations were resolved in other ways. In some cases, the perpetrator confessed and voluntarily surrendered credentials. In other cases, a punishment was defined and carried out.

The United Methodist Church has defined a number of possibilities for handling the situation where charges of sexual misconduct are filed. At the end of the discussion, Swenson added, "When you think about it, there's all the backlash for LGBT issues now, but each of my sexual misconduct charges were followed up, and all but one were heterosexual issues. Only one of them was same gender, the other forty-six were heterosexual." The women bishops did not shirk the difficult work of addressing the church's behavior around sexual ethics. Most have not evaded the discussion of gender, sexual identity, and sexual orientation that consumes the church in the twenty-first century either.

For the earliest women who served as bishops, power and its relationship to patriarchy were related to the rise in consciousness of the ethics of sexual interaction. Bishop Sharon Brown Christopher coined the term, *homosapiensial power*, and differentiated it from institutional power:

> Institutional power is built around control, authority, and hierarchy, and being right all the time. *Homosapiensial* power has something to do with being an integrative person, being authentic, hearing one another, reading the group, and responding to what is true there, rather than what the system has put in place. Isn't the institutional leadership the product of patriarchy? And that's the environment that surrounds us. It's like the fish is swimming in a bowl and can't live without water, but they don't know it, and they don't have a name for it. They don't know that we all swim in that water. And women have begun to name the water. The metaphor doesn't work completely. But I'm wondering if it's a product of patriarchy and the way we are enculturated as children, you know, boys are strong; girls are sweet and nice and pretty.

Patriarchy may be the water we swim in, but many can name it now and long to find a new, more just medium in which to swim.

Women who serve as bishops claim authority and are change agents of that institutional power. Their leadership, at times, ruptured the institutional system and took power away from it. They created these ruptures in order to bring integrity to the whole, or as Bishop Hassinger said, "I hear what you're saying, but God is telling me something else." Bishop Kiesey summed it up: "The church is not necessarily always in the right direction, but faithfulness is. Being able to hear what I believe is Christ's call in the midst of a church that sometimes loses its way, and to return to what I feel Christ has called us to, is what sustains me."

The women bishops also shared stories of times they were wrong and publicly apologized, as well as times when they changed their minds after listening to God and to the church. Some of them were criticized for admitting they were wrong or apologizing. But they argue that those times have not undermined their authority. The confidence that one is called and that the call has been affirmed by the church allows these women to lead with authenticity and humility.

When women began to offer themselves for election as bishops and took office, they brought commitments to collegiality that resulted in new ways of setting up rooms, conducting meetings, and making decisions. They sought to live authentically and to be sensitive to those on the margins. They sought to keep the church on the track that they believed God was calling it to. Sexual ethics charges were taken seriously. Changing to round tables for meeting of the Council of Bishops is a symbol of the approach to claiming authority that entered into the church with the election of women to the episcopacy. "In some ways," says Morrison, "I think we gave permission for men to be who they really were too. Or they gave us permission. I'm sure it was more mutual." She continued, "It was joy-filled." There was a change from straight-line decision making and leadership to a freer, more participative style of leadership. Bishop Mary Ann Swenson described it as

a style of leadership that was about mutuality rather than hierarchy and patriarchy—a style of leadership that valued the people. One of the preachers said to me one time, "We always knew you loved us. We may have disagreed with some of the things that you would do in your time of administration, but we knew you loved us."

Perhaps that was part of the authentic change that women brought to the episcopacy. Women who serve as bishops claim authority and are change agents with love.

Notes

1. Jay Newton-Small, "What Happens When Women Reach a Critical Mass of Influence," *Time Magazine* (November 20, 2017): 21.

2. *The Flyer*, 6, no. 3 (August 1984): 5.

3. *The Flyer*, 4.

4. *The Flyer*, 5.

5. Craig, *Leading*, 167.

6. Judith Craig, ed., *The Leading Women: Stories of the First Women Bishops of The United Methodist Church* (Nashville: Abingdon Press: 2004), 160.

7. Karoline M. Lewis, *She: Five Keys to Unlock the Power of Women in Ministry* (Nashville: Abingdon Press, 2016), 164.

8. Patricia Broughton, "The Church Moves Toward Wholeness: Who Made Our Sister Bishop?" *The Flyer*, 2, no. 4 (August 31, 1980):2.

9. Bruce Ough, http://www.umc.org/who-we-are/the-church-is-watching-waiting-umc-bishops-told, accessed April 30, 2018.

10. Email from Cecelia Long, September 20, 2018. Used with permission.

Five

THE UNIQUE AND HEAVY BURDEN
OF BEING THE FIRST AND MAKING HISTORY

"To be the first is to carry unique and heavy burdens along with the thrill and wonder of making history," wrote Bishop Judith Craig.[1] Craig knew the thrill and wonder well: "I was an early clergywoman in East Ohio. I was probably the first woman Council director, at least in East Ohio. And when I was elected bishop, I was the first everywhere I went." Craig believed that being the first was significant: "When our dust is dust, they'll remember us as those who did the first thing." She also said, "God is doing a new thing. We, by our very presence, have started the chaos." The addition of women to the Council of Bishops meant some revision of assumptions about authority and leadership; the challenges to traditions may have seemed chaotic as the changes occurred. Bishop Susan Morrison mused, "To be claimed for a time such as this in the role I was in, and the ability to touch lives is unbelievable. I'm awestruck." So, those who were the first were learning along with the church that God was calling women to be leaders, even at the level of the episcopacy.

Bishop Linda Lee was aware that she was making history. She was the first African American woman bishop in the North Central Jurisdiction: "I felt like I was representing all African American women everywhere. Because of that, I had to maintain the role in a certain way that would honor the role so that others could come behind me. I didn't want to mess it up for them." The implicit question that many of the bishops experienced is, 'Is she going to be able to hold it steady?'

In 2005, Bishop Rosemarie Wenner was elected out of Germany, a central conference. She was the first woman bishop outside of the United States. Bishop Sharon Rader had been sent to preside. Wenner saw it as "God's struggle," and understood that the Council of Bishops' choice to send a woman bishop to preside provided a model that helped in her election. The voting delegates were asking whether the church was ready for a woman bishop. Wenner responded, "How can we know if we don't try?" The voters in that episcopal election, faithful church members, were willing to try.

Firsts are continuing to happen, even after thirty-six years! Bishop Tracy Smith Malone, elected eleven years after Wenner, in 2016, was still making history as the first in each of her pastoral and conference appointments. Some of the women bishops we interviewed were the first women elected from their conference or the first woman to lead an episcopal area.[2] Some were the first women of color elected in their jurisdiction or serving in an episcopal area. Being a *first* carries with it pressure and scrutiny. While it is also ground breaking and a movement toward wholeness and justice, being a *first* may threaten one's safety, adversely affect one's health, or leave one lonely.

The General Conference granted full clergy rights to women in 1956. It was twenty-four more years before the first woman was elected to the episcopacy. But in 1980, when Matthews was elected, very few women were pastors of larger congregations, let alone bishops. Those women who were elected in the earliest years had almost no models of women leading the church. Those who blazed trails as the *firsts* have carried a unique and heavy burden.

Perhaps the most significant *first* for Christendom was when the first woman bishop put her hands on a candidate in the ritual of ordination. This happened in 1981 at the Wisconsin annual conference. In *The Flyer*, Bishop Sharon Brown Christopher, who was then a district superintendent and present on the platform with a first-row seat, recalls: "Suddenly there was this woman (Matthews) laying hands on and ordaining. It was the first time I had seen a woman ordain a pastor. What happened to me internally was this huge shift. It's like, I *do* belong in the center of the church's life. Women belong at the center of the church's life because ordination is at the center." Bishop Marjorie Matthews was the first woman to ordain clergy for the church.

Consecration of bishops is a holy and unique moment that follows election of bishops in a jurisdictional conference. Following Judith Craig's election, Matthews participated in the consecration service for the North Central Jurisdiction. A woman bishop consecrating a woman bishop was another significant first! Bishop Christopher, who was elected in 1988 in the same jurisdiction, remembers her own consecration:

> The moment of consecration, the kneeling, the bishops' laying on of hands ... became one of those holy moments. Bishops were processing by, and each one was laying on hands, and they were murmuring things. They were saying things, so there was this hum and the shuffle of feet. And I could see the bottoms of their black robes. It was one of those really incredible communal experiences of the whole and a movement of Spirit.

Craig had been consecrated by a college of bishops that included Marjorie Matthews, and Christopher was consecrated by a college that included Judith Craig. Cracks were forming in the patriarchy with these firsts.

In most cases, the women who have been elected bishops of the church are seen as offering something to the church that has been missing or needed. Bishop Sharon Rader brought teaching skills to the episcopacy. Other women bishops are lawyers, pastoral counselors, and theologians, and they bring those experiences and skills along into the office. Bishop Linda Lee brought her practices of spiritual formation and spiritual direction to the Wisconsin Conference. These gifts were different from the relational, administrative style of earlier bishops, and they were resisted at first. People wanted her to be more authoritative and orderly. But she used her spiritual gifts, and the church learned from that. Other women have been elected who are trusted to bring marginalized voices to the table of the church at its highest levels. Bishop Sue Haupert-Johnson brought a deep appreciation for those who serve as local pastors. They trusted her to represent them at the table. Bishop Minerva Carcaño was the first woman of Hispanic heritage to be elected bishop. Bishop Leontine Kelly was the first African American. And another

African American woman was not elected for sixteen years! Bishop Joaquina Nhanala is the first woman bishop elected to an African conference. Bishop Karen Oliveto is the first openly gay bishop: "I represent a whole community that's never been openly present at the bishops' table before. I feel the weight of that," she says. It is a heavy weight. This list could go on and on.

The first husband of a woman bishop was the Rev. Charles Christopher. Bishop Sharon Brown Christopher was the fifth woman elected to the episcopacy, but the first who was accompanied by a husband. She had given herself to "practice the spiritual discipline of itinerancy. I gave myself at my ordination to the church, to be assigned where the church wanted me to serve. . . . If the church wanted to assign me to the episcopacy, I needed to pay attention to that." Her marriage presented new situations for the church to confront. Many traditions had developed for honoring the bishop's wife, but they were not appropriate for a bishop's husband; no corsages were needed! Many of the women bishops' spouses continued in their own ministries and professions, and were unable to travel constantly with their wives and accompany them for the numerous ceremonial occasions that bishops' spouses were expected to attend. Clergy couples all over the church watched to see how this would work.

One of the burdens of the episcopal office is an expectation and need for bishops to spend significant time and energy in travel, in their area and beyond. Bishop Matthews, as the first woman, was particularly in demand across Wisconsin and the worldwide Church. She spoke at many convocations and conferences. She traveled, preaching near and far. Records of the Wisconsin Conference show that Matthews asked the conference in 1983, to fund a part-time position of assistant to the bishop so that, even when she was not present, the office could remain functional and perhaps be helpful to the next person who would serve as bishop in Wisconsin. Her travels made it difficult for her to be in the office even three days a week. Apparently, there was a spirited discussion, but the measure passed. Most of the bishops now have an assistant such as the one Matthews sought.

Not surprisingly, many of the women bishops spoke of times that they were very weary. Bishop Sally Dyck said, "I've often felt like an indentured servant," because of all the events she is expected to attend and tasks she is required to do. Giving oneself permission not to attend or not to do a task is something that the women spoke of as an essential survival mechanism. Still, as Bishop Fierro Harvey said, "I don't want to let anybody down. And mostly I don't want to let myself down." These women have to be tough. They do what needs to be done.

A major effect of the unique and heavy burden is manifested in these women's health. Of the first eight elected, six developed cancer. Matthews had cancer before her election, but it recurred, and she lived only two years after retirement. A public acknowledgment of a bishop's breast or ovarian cancer frequently left others uncomfortable. Each bishop handled it in her own way, but all were honest with the people in their episcopal area that they were going through treatment. Bishop Rader was still recovering from breast cancer surgery when the annual conference meeting occurred in 1995. She realized that she needed to share her situation with the annual conference:

So, we got to lunchtime, and I just stopped and said, I want to take a few minutes before lunch to share with you some of my life story. And I told them. We went to lunch, and when we came back, somebody, I never knew who, some-bodies went out and bought six hundred little safety pins and cut six hundred little pink ribbons (symbol of the fight against breast cancer) and tied them on the safety pins, and everybody had one on when we came back from lunch. I was in tears. Then people started standing up and saying, "Thank you for telling your story. Now I can tell mine to people I have never told." And then the men stood up and said, "It's not just about women with breast cancer. Men need to be telling each other about the cancers they are going through." It was like, "You don't have to go through this alone, Sharon." It was about community.

Bishop Craig had a similar experience. "After the surgery, when I had a bad recovery moment, somebody came in and told me there were prayer chains for me in Germany and in Africa and all around the world. It was like this air mattress was put under me. I floated on that for a long time. I was stunned." Bishop Morrison remembers how supported she was. "I remember, too, the time I was to go into surgery, the whole area had set up this prayer thing. I swear to God, I was still awake, but I floated into the surgery." Morrison is pretty clear that the health challenges are connected to the stress of being firsts. "They didn't slay us, but they nicked us," she commented.

In 2012, the General Board of Pensions and Health Benefits gathered women bishops in order to "gain an understanding of female clergy health issues and barriers to health and well-being" because their data indicated many female clergy were struggling to stay healthy.[3] The bishops named the pressures that they experienced and that they saw female clergy experiencing too. These included the stress of charting a new course as a clergywoman while experiencing the "tyranny (subtle but present) of an anti-woman mind-set and gender bias."[4] The data from health insurance claims makes it clear that this *tyranny* has a physical component and results in such things as obesity, cancer, and other stress-related illnesses. Even the congratulatory hugs could take their toll. Several bishops remembered times they were bruised and sore from hugs!

Answering God's call to ministry as a woman continues to carry unique and heavy burdens. Women are at risk of being threatened, demeaned, and dismissed by the old patriarchal assumptions still alive in some quarters. Stress takes it out on your body. The women bishops are learning to recognize this danger and take steps to counter it, putting down burdens periodically to maintain balance and health. One active bishop wrote on social media about her high stress level; several days of vacation were needed before the stress even began to subside. Clergy women (and men) must take their sabbaths. Renewal leave is available every four years. Too few clergy (or bishops) are doing this, but it is essential in order to maintain physical, spiritual, and emotional health when ministry has unique and heavy burdens.

The daily lives of bishops are demanding because of so many meetings, crises to address, and leadership needed. We heard a variety of ways to address health and wholeness daily. Sally Dyck says she protects the time before 7:30 or 8:00 in the morning: "Before I go to work, I have done Bible study, prayer, a little bit of looking at what the headline news is. I run for about forty-five minutes. And I spend a little time with Ken [her husband]. Then I feel like I have done my self-care, and I can give my life to others." Debra Wallace-Padgett has identified four things that she needs to do every day to feel balanced. She exercises, writes for an hour, experiences a spiritual formation time, and has a "quality conversation" with her husband. With those four activities, she has found balance in the episcopal office; all four must be part of the day, even when she is traveling. Hope Morgan Ward has encouraged her entire episcopal area to address clergy health in both conferences she has led: "We immediately started working on wellness and health. It was a real blessing, because we were all working on it for eight years." Bishop Oliveto has added boxing to her workout routine. "I'm carrying so much in my body. I've just got to get it out," she said. Bishop Wallace-Padgett hits "the daylights out of a racquetball." Others spoke of having a spiritual director, a coach, a therapist, or a personal trainer. Intentional time with one's spouse, family, and long-time friends were also named by virtually every bishop. The bishops are all readers; reading is part of self-care as well as a time to learn. Bishop Dyck walks to work, listens to audible books, and uses public transportation whenever possible as she travels from place to place in the conference. Bishop Fierro Harvey commented that a requirement for bishops is to have "a high threshold for pain." The burdens of serving as bishop require sustained attention to health and wholeness.

Bishop Christopher is convinced that the church has an "underbelly," and the women bishops have experienced it. The attacks and negative activity that come from the underbelly take their toll on leaders. Some of it is in the form of gossip. "People who are newer on the scene, who are not viewed as the norm, both in assignment and in election, are more vulnerable to that kind of general gossip," Sherer said. A man in her jurisdiction actually sent a letter to the members of a General Conference delegation, saying that women and African Americans are in leadership positions only because they're given preferential treatment. Sherer remembered that he wrote, "As long as I'm head of the delegation, I'll be damned if one of *them* will serve us." This openly racist, sexist resistance is important, because it illustrates the prejudice that sometimes manifests in the church, but it is also important to recognize that it exacts a toll on its targets.

Bishop Morrison experienced strong resistance, focused on her feminist commitments. She attended the Re-Imagining Conference in 1993, and was brought up on charges. A friend who was watching the controversy said, "Watch your back. I'm worried about your safety." Bishop Craig was threatened too. She told of a letter that came to the conference office that said they "had better watch out at conference time. There would be a gun and a dead person." Bishop Swenson remembered, "I was hosting the General Conference in Denver, and a gunshot shattered the car window in my driveway." These incidents are from more than twenty years ago, but it is not over. Because of threats to her safety, the FBI was contacted when Bishop Moore-KoiKoi was elected. Bishop Oliveto is often accompanied by a security guard. Bishop Steiner Ball has received threats. Thirty-eight years after the first woman bishop was elected, the resistance continues to take many forms.

The women who serve as bishops also have families and friends and other significant relationships that make demands on their time and energy. Bishop Hassinger recalls personal transitions and issues, such as an adult child who needed help, her divorce, a fractured hip, the death of her parents within ten months of each other, the birth of a grandchild, and treatment for cancer—all of which happened in the first five years of her episcopacy. In retrospect, she wonders how she managed all that. Other bishops have been dealing with aging parents or the death of parents. Children of bishops are not immune to struggle and losing their way. Bishops are human beings with relationships that they cherish and hearts that break.

Bishop Hope Morgan Ward described the challenge of being assigned to a new conference. Many clergy have spent their entire professional lives in one annual conference and never lived anywhere else. They have deep roots. In addition, they know how the culture works there and have colleagues they can trust. When they are sent to a new area, they may know only a few people. They don't know the churches. They have to learn new geography and new communities. They must be on guard, because they have not yet discovered what Bishop Christopher called the underbelly. And they inherit a Cabinet (district superintendents who work with them) that another bishop has appointed. Male bishops face this same challenge, of course. Yet, for many of these women, leadership is very relational. In a new area where they are strangers, relationships may be tentative and take time to deepen. It is lonely. They must learn where the churches are, get to know the clergy and lay leaders, discover the culture and its unwritten rules, and learn to trust the Cabinet. The process also requires being alert to the underbelly. Adjusting to the new conference is lonely work at times.

In addition, bishops are responsible for ordering the whole church. As recently as 2018, two constitutional amendments, which forbade discrimination in The United Methodist Church on the basis of gender, did not accumulate the required two-thirds majority of votes cast in the global church. Women were surprised and appalled at this outcome. Much consternation was expressed, and one of the amendments was returned to the annual conferences for another vote. The women bishops issued a powerful statement in response:

> Like Rachel weeping for her children, so we as episcopal leaders weep for our church. We weep for the physical, mental, emotional, and spiritual harm that is inflicted upon women and girls because of this action. We weep for those who are denied the ability to use their gifts to make a difference in the world. We also weep for those who are not protected from exclusion in the church because of race, color, gender, national origin, ability, age, marital status, or economic condition.
>
> We see you. We weep with you. We seek your healing. We work for the healing of our church. We strive for a church and world that honors every person as a beloved child of God, made in the image of our Creator.[5]

The United Methodist Church, which has spoken out on many justice issues, is an imperfect institution. It has competing forces within, and there is still much work to do before it honors every person as a beloved child of God, made in the image of our Creator. While it advocates for justice everywhere, it must also look to its own processes.

Every female bishop speaks passionately of cultivating a sustaining spirituality as part of the antidote to the heavy burdens of the office. Bishop Wallace-Padgett expressed what many of the women emphasized: That spiritual health is essential. She relies on a team that she has built. "When those really hard moments come . . . of the pain that's almost so deep that you can't even articulate it, I have trouble praying and focusing on Scripture. But knowing that there are other people praying for me, and being able to draw from the well that is so deep—that was developed before that moment came—is a source of real strength."

I dream of

A new kind of bishop

Breath of spring in the sameness of solemn black

Dancing bishop in bright liturgical caftan

Breaking for communion the bread she has baked

Visiting oppressed nations as one who knows what it
    means to be oppressed

A mother figure to her ministers

Ordaining young women and also young men

Singing, acting out a sermon

Nurturing the church to communicate God's love

Writing, speaking in a fresh idiom

A new prophetic voice for the freedom of all people.[6]

Sue Ralph's poem was published in 1976. Much of what she envisioned is embodied by the women bishops, but we must never take lightly the price that these women have paid and continue to pay for the unique and heavy burden of being first. Sue Ralph's dream may be coming true, but not without some suffering.

Notes

1. Judith Craig, ed., *The Leading Women: Stories of the First Women Bishops of The United Methodist Church* (Nashville, Abingdon Press, 2004), 10.

2. See Appendix B for a list.

3. Female Bishops' Focus Group Discussion Summary, Center for Health, General Board of Pension and Health Benefits of The United Methodist Church, June 2012 (for information only/ not for distribution).

4. Female Bishops' Focus Group Discussion Summary.

5. *A Pastoral Letter to the People of The United Methodist Church from the Women Bishops*, May 7, 2018, Council of Bishops, The United Methodist Church. This letter was unanimously affirmed by the entire Council of Bishops.

6. "A Dream" by Sue Ralph in *Images: Women in Transition*. Compiled by Janice Grana. Copyright © 1976. Used by permission of Upper Room Books. upperroombooks.com.

Six

SISTERHOOD AND SUPPORT

In 1992, I (Crain) was a lay delegate to the South Central Jurisdictional Conference. We had six bishops to elect that year. I was excited that this could present an opportunity to elect women and people of color in order to diversify the College of Bishops in that jurisdiction. In the Missouri Episcopal Area, we had two conferences, East and West, but the delegations often met together to consider how various proposals would affect our churches, and to discuss who we might support for bishop. Issues related to sexual orientation were on my radar but not spoken about openly in the delegation. I remember very clearly the day the Rev. Ann Brookshire Sherer flew into Columbia, Missouri, and came to the church where I was serving to meet with the delegations. Her visit was part of our discernment of who we might support for bishop in the voting at jurisdictional conference. Sherer's experiences seemed to prepare her for the world as I saw it, and the church as it should be: with diversity of gender, race, and ethnicity. Sherer had lived as a white woman in African American culture and experienced being a minority. She was serving a multicultural congregation with multiple languages. She was theologically articulate and progressive. I was very excited about our delegation's interest in electing her as a bishop.

I was also fascinated to observe and begin to participate in the political processes. Much discussion revolved around another candidate from the Missouri

West conference, Albert Frederick Mutti. We eventually covenanted to support "Fritz" on several ballots, after much discussion about how earlier delegations had not adhered to a similar covenant. Hurt feelings were aired. I was amazed at the depth of engagement.

I also observed the power of the United Methodist Women (UMW). The women who were part of UMW, as I was, knew one another, because we gathered at the district and conference level regularly; several were effective leaders in the Missouri delegations. UMW meetings raised our consciousness about issues of inclusion and justice. I particularly remember being introduced to "Help Us Accept Each Other" (now #560 in *The United Methodist Hymnal*) at a conference gathering in the early 1980s. I was moved by its message of inclusion. We were certain that the church would be improved by including women in leadership at the highest levels. United Methodist Women was spreading this message of encouragement to women in annual conferences around The UMC. The Rev. Anita Wood, active in the West Ohio Conference, recalls that whoever was currently serving as the UMW conference president was always elected as a delegate to General and/ or Jurisdictional Conference from West Ohio in that decade. United Methodist Women were organized and intentional about equipping their participants, laywomen, for leadership and in support of women clergy.

Women with particular gifts for leadership were lifted up, and issues of concern to women were discussed. In the 1970s, conference-level officers of United Methodist Women (UMW) "caucused every time they got together. They were concerned in general with women's issues but also hoped to see a woman elected as bishop," recalls Barbara Campbell, who was a staff member of the Women's Division for almost forty years. Campbell is careful to clarify that these caucus meetings were not organized by the Women's Division. They were informally gathered meetings that brought together women who were part of the voting delegates. "Those women, who had been identified as leaders by UMW and elected to their conference delegations, knew each other and worked together for women's issues," she said.

"They were working like crazy around Marjorie's [Matthews] candidacy. They were excited and confident," Campbell remembers. The Women's Division was also cooperating with GCSRW to sponsor training "to get women more active in the church. If you want to get elected [to Annual or General and Jurisdictional Conference], this is how you do it!" Campbell is clear that these trainings "opened what had been sort of under the table, known only to those in the *good ole boys club*. This knowledge had never been public, so women had to be taught how to organize and get elected."

United Methodist Women was also influential through its system of gathering in order to teach and inspire women in their mission work. Campbell described how inviting a clergywoman with potential for episcopal leadership to preach or teach at conference UMW events or School of Missions could advance her recognition: "This was informal. No announcements would be made that Rev. So-and-so, who will be the speaker for the event, is running for bishop. Yet the organizers knew and invited those whom they saw as potential bishops." Bishop Rader recalls being told by an organizer of such an event that they frequently invited leadership they believed might one day be a bishop. This kind of informal support could make an enormous difference and was needed, because clergywomen were still very rarely appointed to larger churches or as district superintendents.

Campbell described two examples of "symbolic places where you could make a point without saying anything. In 1972, clergywomen were invited to conduct the closing worship of the national UMW Assembly held in Cincinnati, Ohio. In 2018, women bishops were invited to conduct the closing worship of the national Assembly, including Bishop Karen Oliveto, the first openly gay bishop." This informal advocacy signaled acceptance. The Assembly is a large national event that draws women from all across the church. "In 1982, Bishop Marjorie Matthews was invited to be the UMW Assembly speaker. That year, the Assembly conflicted with the Council of Bishops spring meeting. At first, the Council said no, that Bishop Matthews could not miss the Council meeting. But they relented, and she was the Assembly speaker." Campbell's recollection illustrated the growing power of women in the church, and the support that UMW gave to the ordination of women in the first decades and to women in the episcopacy.

The decades of the 1970s and 1980s were times of pushing for the rights of women. The Equal Rights Amendment was under discussion. Women, lives changed by the birth control pill, were seeking to rewrite the rules for marriage partnerships; some husbands were even expected to iron their own shirts and change diapers! Meanwhile, a push was on in the church to involve women at all levels of decision-making and leadership, including serving as pastors and bishops. Laywomen were very active in these efforts, as were the growing critical mass of clergywomen.

Four years after the 1968 merger of The Methodist Church and the Evangelical United Brethren, the newly formed The United Methodist Church created the General Commission on the Status and Role of Women, which was to monitor and advocate for the status of women in the denomination. GCSRW, or COSROW as it came to be called, was concerned with both lay- and clergywomen. It formed partnerships with the Women's Division of the General Board of Global Ministries (the home of UMW) and with the General Board of Higher Education and Ministry, which was tasked with supporting clergywomen.

The new commission, GCSRW, began by modeling a collaborative way of leadership for the denomination when it chose to have a general secretariat, shared by two women. In 1973, Nancy Grissom Self and Judith Leaming Elmer became the first "secretariat," a radical departure from earlier denominational practice of choosing one person as general secretary for each of its national boards. Self and Elmer shared the position. By 1991, the secretariat expanded to three.[1] This "put three women at the table of general secretaries. Women could be seen and known where they had not been," according to the Rev. Stephanie Anna Hixon, who was part of the secretariat (1991–2004). The commission was also intentional in choosing diverse women for the secretariat. All of the other general agencies had traditionally had one general secretary at their head, and nearly all had been men.

At the outset, Nan Self took on the task of advocating for both lay- and clergywomen in leadership. She had an eye for those with special gifts and would suggest to them they might consider making themselves available to the church. Several of the first women who were elected as bishops mention Self as a critically important encourager and enabler of their coming to the attention of the jurisdictions and eventually being elected.

In the last thirty years of the twentieth century, GCSRW, Women's Division (administrative home for United Methodist Women), and the General Board of Higher Education and Ministry (GBHEM), which was concerned in part with supporting clergywomen, all had a hand in lifting up women who were potential leaders or bishops, and helping women learn to navigate the United Methodist system of conferences. Just providing opportunities for women to get together was an important strategy of these groups. The Rev. Stephanie Hixon identified these gatherings as a "place to magnify the voice" of women. Many of the earliest women bishops were identified and inspired by the clergywomen's gatherings sponsored by GCSRW and GBHEM. The 1975 Clergywomen's Consultation, which dared to imagine that a woman could be a bishop, was one of these, as was the Black Clergywomen's group. United Methodist Women trained laywomen about how the political processes of the church worked, how to get elected as a General and Jurisdictional Conference delegate, and also provided ways for women to get to know one another. Women were inspired to step forward and claim their skills as leaders. In addition, they often invited clergywomen with special gifts as leaders to speak at their gatherings and educational events, and in this way, laywomen came to know possible candidates for election as bishops.

By 1992, these training opportunities for women had been formalized, assisting women to grow stronger in the church's decision-making bodies. Training happened in many annual conferences, and also at General Conference every four years. At the General Conference, an event was generally held before the formal convening of the Conference and the legislative committees began their work. Women who might be nominated as officers of legislative committees were introduced, and legislative issues particularly related to women were highlighted. This training event was empowering and clarifying. Hixon remembers that some criticized the training as "manipulative," but the discussion was open to all those who showed up and wished to address the gathering.

The advocacy and training that UMW sponsored focused on laywomen, and dated back to the early years of the twentieth century. Deaconess Barbara Campbell remembered that the Woman's Missionary Council of the southern church had taken on these issues as early as the 1920s. They sent resolutions to the General Conference repeatedly, and the resolutions for full inclusion of women continued after the union of the northern and southern churches in 1939. They had a national committee, and each local church women's group was urged to include an office called "status of women."

Other women who were particularly important in the earliest years were the Rev. Jeanne Audrey Powers, the Rev. Barbara Troxell, Dr. Diedre Kriewald, and Joanne Miles; but Nancy Grissom Self stands above them all. She was the force behind the movement that began to elect women as bishops and to encourage all clergywomen to take authority and lead. They were aided by communications such as *WellSprings, A Journal for United Methodist Clergywomen*, published by the Section of Elders and Local Pastors, Division of Ordained Ministry, General Board of Higher Education and Ministry of The United Methodist Church.[2] *The Yellow Ribbon* was a newsletter put together by the women's caucus. Phyllis Tholin and Peggy Garrison gave major energy to it. The General Commission on the Status and Role of Women began publishing *The Flyer*, which told of action at the general church level as well as reporting on each annual conference. Women across the church could sign up to receive *The Flyer*. Names of women one needed to know were on those pages, along with notice of places to gather. Most of this organizing and communicating was begun by women to fill needs rather than coming down from the agencies. It was grassroots organizing at its best.

In 2016, four US jurisdictions elected seven women bishops. That is the most elected in one year, and it happened in the sixtieth year after women were granted full clergy rights in the denomination. In the Southeast, a symbol of the journey in the form of a broken pottery pitcher and bowl was brought to the jurisdictional conference by retired Bishop Charlene Kammerer. The pottery had been purchased in the 1980s, by women of the jurisdiction who hoped that the jurisdictional conference would elect the Rev. Helen Crotwell. That election did not happen, and the pottery was broken in transit. Crotwell did not repair the pottery but decided instead to keep it until a woman could be elected at a future conference. When Kammerer was elected in 1996, the pitcher and bowl were mended, with Kammerer guiding Crotwell's hands. These pieces have become holy to the women of the jurisdiction, as they symbolize the healing of the body that came through including women in its leadership. "Helen's spirit is with us today," Kammerer said. "She is in the heavenly kingdom with Leontine and many others."[3] Women have kept the goal of full participation alive for many years now. It has not yet been fully realized, but women continue to work together toward that goal.

From 1972 to the present, opportunities for women to gather together and encourage one another, strategize, and identify women who should be offered as leaders have remained important. United Methodist Women continue to lead the denomination in its attention to justice issues for women and children. The General Board of Higher Education and Ministry has a staff position to support clergywomen and sponsors occasional gatherings. The General Commission on the Status and Role of Women joins with the General Commission on Religion and Race to monitor the denominational inclusion of women, people of color, and others who are marginalized. Their reports serve to keep justice and inclusion always before us. They report whose voices are heard, who is present in decision-making, and who is missing.

In addition, GCSRW has kept the denomination's attention on sexual ethics. They provide training. They also offer advice to anyone considering making a charge of sexual misconduct. Their statistical reports, advocacy, programing, and legislation lift up the causes of women. The goals are articulated in this statement:

> We, at The General Commission on the Status and Role of Women, commit ourselves to continue to advocate for women individually and collectively within The United Methodist Church, to work to be a catalyst to redress inequities of the past and to prevent future inequities against women in The United Methodist Church, and to monitor to ensure inclusiveness in the programmatic and administrative functioning of the church by providing resources and support.
>
> As mandated by Christ, let us live fully into the gospel promise that "there is no longer male and female, for all of you are one in Christ Jesus." (Galatians 3:28)[4]

The gatherings and advocacy built a sisterhood that has sustained and supported women in The United Methodist Church. However, being a woman in ministry continues to be stressful and lonely at times. Young clergywomen continue to face sexism along with the struggles of family life. Those women struggle too often to be accepted as professionals and to protect family time. One clergywoman recently shared on social media that she had received criticism for the nursery staffing, even though her husband, who is co-pastor, has responsibility for supervision of that staff. The critical email seemed to assume that, because she was a woman, it was her fault. This kind of thing continues unabated.

The women who have been chosen for the office of bishop have found it to be especially lonely and stressful. They all spoke of how they leaned on other women bishops who could mentor or just understand the challenges of governing an episcopal area. Bishop Violet Fisher talked of how lonely she was after she moved to New York. She finally found a Black church where she felt at home, and would go there for worship when her schedule allowed. It was not a United Methodist church, so she could enjoy a certain amount of anonymity. She had left behind family and friends when she became bishop. Our interviews revealed that the friendship between neighboring sister bishops, Fisher and Morrison, is strong to this day. The interviewing we did for this book was an opportunity for the bishops to share their joys and struggles. As we concluded an interview focus group, Bishop Sally Dyck said, "I feel the deepness, the richness, the connection so much more. We thank you for this evening." Women who are United Methodist bishops continue to need one another.

The women bishops were clear also that they needed to find people who knew them before they were elected or were not part of the church. With these people, they could be themselves. Several spoke of the importance of being with family regularly. None of these women want to harm The UMC, but they do want to be part of bringing the church closer to perfection as promised by God's grace. They are fearful of harming, and they feel the weight. Yet they courageously confront the evil that presents itself. The sisterhood supports and sustains. For nearly all the women bishops, there remains a strong desire and need to connect with their women colleagues; for it is in those times they experience freedom, an ability to speak with others who understand without judgment, and a strong sense of Spirit undergirding their common life and work.

Notes

1. Cecelia Long, Kiyoko Kasai Fujiu, and Stephanie Hixon served together.

2. *The WellSprings Journal* is still in publication. Find it at http://www.wellspringsjournal.org/.

3. http://www.umc.org/news-and-media/new-women-bishops-make-history, accessed April 12, 2018.

4. https://www.gcsrw.org, accessed July 25, 2018.

Seven

HOLDING FAST TO THE VISION: "I'M LIVING TOMORROW TODAY"[1]

The stories in this book span the years from 1980, when the first woman was elected to the episcopacy in The United Methodist Church, to the present. Thirty-four women have become bishops in the last thirty-eight years. The *tomorrow* that many in the church had longed for, where women were full participants in the leadership of the denomination, has begun to manifest. Yet resistance to women clergy and women bishops is still present. The *already* but *not yet* reality requires us to hold fast to the vision, but also to identify and celebrate the moments where we *live tomorrow today*.

These are stories of faith, courage, pain, joy, struggle, and perseverance. These moments, where the church fulfilled the vision of tomorrow, paint a hope-filled picture. They may inspire and guide women who are just now hearing a call to ordained ministry, as well as those who are well along the road. These stories may alert women entering ministry and episcopacy to the yet unfulfilled vision of a church where both men and women fully share ministry and leadership. As the song says,

And the ONES WHO'VE GONE BEFORE US will show us the way,
The ones who follow after will welcome the new day.
And the ONES WHO'VE GONE BEFORE US, will join in the chorus,
When we do, when we make it through.[2]

In 2012, as the Church of England debated the matter of women bishops, Diarmaid MacCulloch, professor of church history at the University of Oxford, wrote:

Christian history shows a consistent pattern from Paul to the present. In times of trial and conflict, or of rapid innovation in theology, men fall away from their accustomed leadership roles, partly because they are more likely than women to be victims of punitive violence from other men. In their place, female leadership re-emerges as a survival strategy for the church. The time for men to take over again is when life has returned to more tranquil patterns, the church conforms once more to the expectations of society around it and the historical record is adjusted to match those expectations.[3]

This historian appears rather pessimistic about the church in the present. The survival of the traditional church is questioned. He welcomes the leadership of women as a "survival strategy" until the church *conforms* [author's emphasis] to the "expectations of society around it."[4] This is a surprising expectation. Does the church conform to the society, or should the church lead the culture? Society/culture of the 1960s and 1970s seethed with the pressure of the women's movement. The church was not immune to that pressure. As possibilities for women opened in other professions, they opened in The UMC. Many women and men in both church and culture welcomed these new opportunities. Others resisted loudly and persistently. Culture and church are intertwined, each influenced by the other. Importantly, The United Methodist Church led mainstream protestant denominations in welcoming women to its highest levels of leadership.

The shift to more egalitarian practices in The UMC has continued. A quota system now ensures that committees and commissions include diverse membership. We attend to race, gender, and geographic representation, along with a balance of clergy and laity. Other changes reflect the diversity of The UMC. The central conferences (those outside the United States) have grown, and their representation has impacted the makeup of the General Conference. The ranks of white men that were present in 1968 are replaced by diverse people from Africa, Europe, the Philippines, and the United States. Central conference delegates vote alongside delegates from the United States. A wide variety of theologies, cultures, languages, and life experiences is present. This diversity is rich, challenging, and insistent as the church lives into its vision for discipleship and transformation.

The effects of rapid change in the denomination, particularly in the United States, are both positive and negative. On the negative side, the church seems to be slipping in membership in the United States; millennials, particularly, are not finding the church compelling enough to attend. The deep divide found in American culture between conservative and progressive values is replicated in the church. On the positive side, liberation theologies that include the voices from the margins have taken root through our hymns, liturgies, Christian education, and preaching; they add perspective and variety to the traditions still anchoring the church. Many experiments in new faith communities are underway. The order of deacon, which focuses on ministries of Word, service, compassion, and justice, has brought the ministry of *diakonia* into the center of the church's life, and millennials and other young people are attracted to its missional focus. The United Methodist Church continues to try to invite and respond to newer generations. Persons of all ages are excited about giving their lives to causes that bring about change and move toward justice and inclusion. Diverse voices demand to be heard. God continues to call the church to justice and wholeness. While there may be some, like MacCulloch, who would argue that the diminishing of numbers in The United Methodist Church in the US can be partially blamed on the emergence of women clergy and bishops in the last half of the twentieth century, that blame is misplaced. The shift in Western culture toward secularism is powerful and must not be overlooked as a cause of the shrinking numbers of United Methodists. We do not believe the church can or will revert to those earlier patriarchal patterns.

In addition, the hidden practices that supported white privilege in the United States and Europe are being revealed. The backlash is strident, but both church and culture are becoming sensitized to the demonic power of white privilege. The litany, written as a companion to the United Methodist Social Creed, says, "God embraces all hues of humanity, / delights in diversity and difference, / favors solidarity transforming strangers into friends."[5] The movement to include women as episcopal leaders must extend to confront white privilege and other unjust systems.

In 2018, some clergywomen confronted it. Abingdon Press published a collection of prayers written by clergywomen, *We Pray With Her: Encouragement for All Women Who Lead*. The Rev. Emily Peck-McClain was one of the editors. After its publication, the book was criticized by some because its editorial team was all white, and it contained only a few pieces by women of color. Peck-McClain responded, "We deserve to be criticized about this. . . . We are not done and must continue to do the work we are called to do, which includes dismantling white supremacy."[6] Young clergywomen are in the forefront of this justice work.

Now we come to an important question: What was it about *these* women bishops that enabled them to persevere, claim authority, define leadership in their own ways, and rise to the episcopacy? To a woman, we heard the self-affirmation and assurance that they were called by God, were affirmed by the church, and had found and were finding true meaning and purpose in their episcopal ministries. Persistence is a result of clarity about God's call. As United Methodists, these women discerned, tested, and claimed the call, through both their personal experiences and the community. The call sustained them. As Bishop Joaquina Nhanala said, "I believe when the plan is from God, it happens." Part of God's plan seems to be to call women such as Rosemarie Wenner into episcopal leadership. "I walk closely with people, and I look carefully at those at the margins," she said. Violet Fisher said, "We all have our place at the table. We all belong to the same body and serve the same God, and there should not be separation at any level." Bishop Matthews said that, if God opened a door, she would walk through it. The call to participate in God's gracious work is powerful, as the ones who've gone before us illustrate.

Answering God's call to ministry as a woman continues to carry unique and heavy burdens. Women are at risk of being threatened, demeaned, and dismissed by the old patriarchal assumptions still alive in some quarters. Many of the women who have been elected to the episcopacy have had cancer. Stress takes it out on your body. We are learning to recognize this danger and take steps to counter it, putting down burdens periodically to maintain balance and health. One active bishop wrote on social media that she realized that it took several days of vacation before her stress level began to subside. Clergywomen (and clergymen) need to model the theological and physical importance of sabbath time, and to observe the renewal leave that is available every four years. Too few clergy (or bishops) are doing this, but it is essential in order to maintain physical, spiritual, and emotional health when ministry has unique and heavy burdens.

In the 1980s and 1990s, the Baltimore-Washington clergywomen "gathered and sang for survival," said Bishop Morrison. Nearly forty years later, the need for connection and community has not abated. One of the antidotes to stress and dis-ease is sisterhood and support. Throughout the last forty-plus years, the national and international gatherings of clergywomen sponsored by the denomination may have had differing emphases, yet they were still welcomed and well attended. Many women bishops and clergy continue to express the need for cultivating community to avoid the risk of burnout and to share common life experiences, language, and cultural realities. Gathering in community renews and encourages the women as they seek to remain faithful to God's claim on their lives.

The UMC provides opportunities to connect with other clergywomen, but sometimes these are too expensive or too large for one to find the sisterhood that is beneficial. Every clergywoman needs a few sisters who will form a covenant group in which she is both nurtured and held accountable. The group's regular gatherings need not be physical; they can use digital conferencing. But this kind of group is essential for health. Such a group demands a covenant to be present to it regularly. Over the years, such a group becomes life-giving.

Closed groups on social media can fulfill some of the need for sisterhood and support. As long as the group is clear about confidentiality, many helpful conversations can occur. One day recently, one of those groups included a clergywoman asking whether she should wear a robe or a gray dress for an outdoor wedding, another seeking prayers for endometriosis, one soliciting suggestions for leading a staff retreat, and several asking for suggestions of curriculum resources for confirmation classes. Another thread on social media invited clergywomen to share the nicknames that demean them: Little Bit, CLAP (cute little assistant pastor), P Mel (Pastor Melissa), and Baby Cakes were some that came up quickly on the feed.[7] Another pastor asked for prayers as she went to visit a woman who had been abused by her spouse. The Rev. Amanda Bennett Baker quickly responded: "Grant that she, and all who have absorbed the lies of abuse, may come to know herself to be your precious beloved child."[8] The conversations are often rich and theological, as well as expressing pain and frustration and offering encouragement.

Change and the relinquishing of position and power are not easily accomplished. Thirty-eight years after Marjorie Matthews became the first woman bishop, the women bishops we interviewed were still experiencing sexism, racism, ageism, harassment, and even abuse. During a Council of Bishops meeting in 2017, the General Commission on the Status and Role of Women led the bishops in additional training regarding sexual ethics. One table of bishops was filled with only women. That table of women admitted to one another and then to the whole Council that every one of them had experienced harassment or abuse during their ministries; for some, that harassment or abuse occurred at Council of Bishops meetings! The church is not yet fully living God's vision for humanity when sexual misconduct continues to demean individuals and the church. Women bishops believe their presence in leadership has allowed and encouraged those who have suffered abuse to come forward to speak of their pain and seek restitution. The women bishops embody hope and courage for those who have been silenced, not believed, or abused. In addition, as women share their experiences of oppression with one another through the #MeToo movement, more women are finding courage to speak up and claim their rightful place. This new openness in the culture may eventuate in more just means of interaction. One can only hope and pray that the voices will continue to be heard. If the women bishops have anything to do with it, they *will* be heard.

Persistence and hope thrive when Christian values are clear. The theological task of claiming that God's love and light includes the whole human race—in all of its diversity—remains urgent. Fifty years ago, women spent considerable time and effort addressing language and images for God. God the *Father* dominated liturgies, prayers, and hymns. Part of the process that opened ordination to women required revisiting concepts of the Holy. Careful searching of Scripture found God described in many ways, including as *mother* and *womb*. Women, too, reflect the image of God. In 2018, that work continues, even as The United Methodist Church engages additional concerns for racial, gender, and sexuality justice. Many are challenging the old binary notions of human as male or female, or marriage as between only a man and woman. Theologians are constructing theologies that encompass the diversity we have come to know in creation. The work of theology today is a work of justice; it is urgent! The ones who've gone before us show us that theological work is essential.

The source and content of the urgency are focused differently than in 1980. White privilege and heterosexism, particularly in the United States, have joined patriarchy in oppressing and injuring the loved ones of God's creation. The UMC takes a stand for inclusion. Leading the church's witness in August 2018 was a woman bishop, LaTrelle Easterling. A "Unite the Right" rally was scheduled in Washington, DC, featuring the hate-driven values of white supremacist groups. In response, Bishop Easterling inspired a "Unite to Love" rally, and fifteen hundred persons assembled. She spoke these words:

> When anyone believes themselves to be superior to others, they betray God; when anyone believes the color of their skin means God favors them over skin of a different hue, they betray God; when anyone passively benefits from racist and discriminatory policies, practices, and programs, they betray God; when anyone silently witnesses the mistreatment of others created in the image and likeness of God based on racist, sexist, xenophobic, and other categories of designed difference, they betray God. ... There is no race but the human race.[9]

Our theological task is urgent in the face of blatant racism, sexism, and other forms of oppression. When asked about the contributions of women in leadership in the church, the bishops we interviewed spoke of the need to: (1) work to eliminate discrimination of women and girls; (2) open full access to a meaningful life; (3) lament the devaluation and discrimination that continues in the church and world; and (4) renew commitments to ensure that all people are treated with respect, compassion, and grace. Bishop Easterling's words at the rally addressed all four.

Sadly, as we interviewed the thirty-two living women bishops, they periodically requested that we turn off the recording machine when a woman began to share a painful time when she had been demeaned, harassed, or denied full use of her voice and ability in her work as a bishop. Women still must decide how much or how often they are willing to confront systems, theologies, and relationships. To confront and challenge is to risk rejection, denial, hurt feelings, public shaming, church complaints, and even silencing. Knowing they are a challenge to "the way it's always been" still causes women, on almost a daily basis, to have to assess when, where, and how they will speak out for justice and challenge oppressive systems. Too often, women bishops still experience loneliness, discouragement, and a sense of "craziness." Is it any wonder the women seem to experience more health complications than their male colleagues?

The leadership style of each woman who is a bishop is unique. The women bishops are initiating and implementing change in diverse ways as they claim authority as leaders. Some are tireless in the work of forming relationships from which flows collaboration and creativity; others are orderly and controlled in their administrative processes, building teams of people to work alongside. Some seek out lots of ideas from others; others begin with solitude and prayer to reveal the next steps for their leadership. Some revel in the chaos and complexities of legislation; others avoid political processes. No doubt, other ways of claiming authority can be found in these women's stories.

Whatever their individual styles and perspectives, the women stressed their reliance on guidance from the Holy Spirit in order to lead authentically from their souls. Every one of these women evidenced this authenticity and encouraged it in others.

The theological understanding of *church* needed stretching as the notion that women could be bishops took hold. The United Methodist Church continues to examine its ecclesiology. The world has become smaller; multiple religions inhabit our communities; evangelism is still our task. But what *is* the good news we need to share in the world as we know it? Surely, we must learn to appreciate and embrace the diversity of God's creation. Our task is to participate in God's mission in the world. We must listen and look for the guidance of the Holy Spirit as we try to discern what God is doing, and then join in with the Divine project.

Concluding the 2018 United Methodist Women's Assembly in Columbus, Ohio, where seven women bishops (and one male bishop) presided over the service of Holy Communion, Executive Secretary Harriett Olson spoke to the women bishops on the platform:

> We are grateful for all the gifts you bring: spiritual wisdom, strength to lead, racial ethnic diversity and with a wide range of gifts. Think about what our church can look like in the future—women and men, diverse in race, ethnicity and experience, working with laity, and committed to the liberation of all who come to the table of grace. . . . We are blessed to hear [your] stories.

The authors of this book have been blessed by the stories and reflections of the thirty-four women who have been elected bishops of The United Methodist Church. As we have listened and learned, we have sensed the movement of the Holy Spirit leading the church (sometimes reluctantly) to embrace the full participation of women willing to offer their lives and ministries so the church and the world might be transformed to the kin-dom of God. Thirty-eight years since the first woman, Marjorie Matthews, was consecrated a bishop of The United Methodist Church does not seem long when one considers the full sweep of history. But it has been a journey that has moved from fear and resistance to ever greater expectation and acceptance. And for that we give God our thanks and praise.

The work for full acceptance of women's leadership in the church is not yet finished. As Bishop Haupert-Johnson shared in a Facebook post on April 13, 2018: "I was criticized by some when I was offered for election as a bishop [in 2016] for being 'pro women' (still puzzles me why they thought that was negative). I might as well live into that characterization, because it is important to my daughter and our daughters everywhere."

The signs of health and wholeness in the church are proliferating. Bishop Cynthia Fierro Harvey described her first ordination service:

The first person I ordained was a woman. And the person who stood with her was the first woman ever ordained in Louisiana. I've got my hands on her head, and Carol Cotton Winn is standing with her, the first woman ordained in Louisiana. Carol came to take Communion with tears in her eyes because she had worked for that moment. They had worked tirelessly for sixteen years to elect another woman bishop. And for them to receive that person was pretty extraordinary.

The United Methodist Church is beginning a second wave of women's leadership. We wrote earlier about reaching critical mass before change can really begin. Women are reaching a critical mass in the Council of Bishops. Clergywomen are reaching critical mass in the five jurisdictions of the US. Change is happening.

These episcopal leaders have a vision for a more just and inclusive church. They see injustice particularly clearly, perhaps because they experience oppression themselves. They are committed to using the power of the episcopal office to teach and be a new vision of the church. Bishops Hassinger, Lee, and Carcaño have offered strong and competent leadership in the Council of Bishops as it has addressed white privilege and racism. Many women bishops have used their power to combat racism, sexism, and heterosexism. Bishop Harvey is poised to become the president of the Council as The UMC lives into decisions of the 2019 Special General Conference. They have stood up to sexual misconduct, even when it meant removing a popular or successful pastor. They have supported the victims of sexual harassment. They have elevated women to positions that were previously closed to them. Yet the stories they shared make it clear that these oppressions continue. Some are directed at the bishop herself. Others are embedded in the culture of the episcopal area. And yet, like Bishop Marjorie Matthews, they "firmly believe that God calls both men and women . . . into the work of the church. God is more interested in persons who are willing to be used in the ministry, or in the work of the church than . . . in the sex of the person."[10]

"There is neither Jew nor Greek; there is neither slave nor free; nor is there male and female, for you are all one in Christ Jesus" (Gal 3:28) wrote Paul in Galatians. Paul's vision of the reign of God has not been fully realized in the

197

church. Yet we see these women holding fast to that vision and doing all in their power to move toward it. In the 1970s and 1980s, the Baltimore clergywomen's group sang this chorus so hopefully:

> O, I'm steppin' out, steppin' out on the promises.
> O, I'm steppin' out, steppin' out all the way.
> O, I'm steppin' out, steppin' out on the promises.
> I'm living tomorrow today.[11]

They longed for a church that welcomed their leadership and honored their calling. They were excited to be—finally—full clergy members of their annual conferences. The stained-glass ceiling was pretty firmly in place. Still they dared to dream of "living tomorrow today" and began to identify the women among them who were good candidates for the episcopacy. They talked to their friends and colleagues. They found many men who also longed for the end of patriarchy and the fulfillment of Paul's inclusive vision. "You are all God's children," said Paul (Gal 3:26). Momentum began to gather. And, in 1980, Marjorie Matthews was elected! Great joy! We must not forget that those clergy voting in 1980 were almost entirely men; very few clergywomen were part of voting delegations. Four years later, two women were elected! Eight years later, Susan Morrison's election was celebrated by the clergywomen in her conference by decorating the statue of John Wesley on the grounds of West Virginia Wesleyan College, where the jurisdiction was voting, with pink streamers. They gathered around the decorated statue before the consecration service and sang their songs. They had stepped out on the promises and felt like they were "living tomorrow" that day!

How does this guide us into the future? The interviews with these wonderful women who have offered themselves to The United Methodist Church reveal several clues for the future. First, our theological task is never complete. We must continue to expand our concept of God and God's will for the world. The United Methodist Church must be more than a corporation or institution; the church is both human and divine. We must continue to seek the guidance of the Holy Spirit in all that we do. All clergywomen and clergymen must continue to attend to their call, their identity, and their authentic humanness as they live into their authority and leadership. The burdens of leadership at the highest level are heavy; bishops must care for body and soul. Most of all, leaders in the church must hold fast to the vision and live into it each day. The ones who've gone before us do show us the way.

"Life is a hard battle anyway," said Sojourner Truth. "If we laugh and sing a little as we fight the good fight of freedom it makes it all go easier. I will not allow my life's light to be determined by the darkness around me."[12] A song that sustained the clergywomen in the 1970s and 1980s, is "I'd Take Nothing for the Journey." The words remind us of the challenges of the journey. But the chorus claims the urgency and joy. Here's the whole song:

Refrain
I'd take nothing for the journey.
I'd take nothing I heard her say
I'd take nothing for the journey
I'd take nothing for the way, for the way.

Our women are crying in the wilderness
Calling out, yet falling through the cracks
Shattered vessels once filled with water
Crowded, empty spaces, burdened backs.

Refrain
As priest, prophet, or pastor
Ancient systems still define our roles,
But we've heard our sisters' stories
Calling us to ministry that's holy whole.

Refrain
Gathering, spinning, and weaving,
Painting pain in glory hues
Mosaics of justice and oppression,
Celebrating art of me, of you.

Refrain[13]

The first women who joined the Council of Bishops in The United Methodist Church gather together with smiles. Like Sojourner Truth, they sing and laugh. Theirs is a calling from God, confirmed by the church, and lived out with joy. There are no regrets. They stepped out on the promises and lived tomorrow even as they encountered the darkness. They affirm that they would "take nothing for the journey." They persisted. The rupture occurred. They live with hope.

Notes

1. This is the last line in the chorus of Susan R. Beehler's "Steppin' Out," as found in *A Shared Journey,* by Janet E. Powers and Susan R. Beehler (Hacienda Springs, Inc., 1984/2002), 67. Tomorrow refers to the vision of a time when women could live their identity and calling fully and freely.

2. "Ones Who've Gone Before Us," words and music by Doris J. Ellzey (Blesoff), © 1975 Doris Ellzey (Blesoff). Used by permission.

3. Diarmaid MacCulloch, "Women bishops: Jesus was happy with female apostles. What is the Church of England's problem?" *The Guardian* (July 7, 2012), https://www.theguardian.com/world/2012/jul/07/female-apostles-fine-for-jesus, accessed August 22, 2018.

4. MacCulloch, "Women bishops."

5. The *Discipline,* ¶166.

6. Emily Peck-McClain, Facebook post, September 7, 2018. Used by permission.

7. Private group posts, Facebook, September 15, 2018.

8. Private group posts, Facebook, September 16, 2018.

9. Bishop LaTrelle Easterling, Washington DC Area, speech given at the August 12, 2018 "Unite to Love" rally. Quoted in Melissa Lauber, "United Methodists Unite to Love," UM Insight (August 15, 2018): 3, https://um-insight.net/in-the-world/advocating-justice/united-methodists-unite-to-love/, accessed October 27, 2018.

10. Marjorie Matthews, interview included in "Early Women Bishops of The UMC (Episcopal Series, Claremont School of Theology, 1984), https://www.youtube.com/watch?v=wHYzKPSZtaY, accessed October 27, 2018.

11. Susan R. Beehler, "Steppin' Out," Beehler and Powers, *A Shared Journey,* 67. Words and music by Susan Beehler. Used by permission.

12. Sojourner Truth, as quoted by Joan Chittister, *The Monastic Way* (March 31, 2018), http:/The Monastic Way.org.

13. Susan Beehler, "I'd Take Nothing for the Journey," Beehler and Powers, *A Shared Journey,* 1–2. Words of the title were shared by the Rev. Daisy Thompson and the song is dedicated to her. Words and music by Susan Beehler. Used by permission.

APPENDICES

Appendix A

INTERVIEWS AND FOCUS GROUPS

Date	Interviews with Bishops
April 11, 2017	Susan Morrison
April 11, 2017	Judith Craig
April 10–11, 2017	Judith Craig, Ann Brookshire Sherer, Mary Ann Swenson, Sharon Brown Christopher, Susan Morrison, Sharon Zimmerman Rader
April 29, 2017	Beverly Shamana, Linda Lee
April 29, 2017	Susan Wolfe Hassinger, Jane Allen Middleton, Janice Riggle Huie, Charlene Payne Kammerer, Deborah L. Kiesey
April 30, 2017	Joaquina Filipe Nhanala, Rosemarie J. Wenner
May 10, 2107	Violet L. Fisher, Susan Morrison
November 4, 2017	Tracy Smith Malone, Cynthia Moore-KoiKoi, Sue Haupert-Johnson, Sandra Lynn Steiner Ball
November 4, 2017	Sally Dyck, Karen Oliveto, Cynthia Fierro Harvey, Deborah Wallace-Padgett, Hope Morgan Ward

November 5, 2017	Minerva G. Carcaño, LaTrelle Easterling, Laurie Haller, Peggy A. Johnson, Sharma Lewis
January 27, 2018	Elaine J. W. Stanovsky, Mary Virginia Taylor

Date	**Other Interviewees**
December 19, 2017	Rev. Barbara Troxell (phone)
June 7, 2018	Rev. Anita D. Wood (phone)
June 22, 2018	Deaconess Barbara Campbell (phone)
June 25, 2018	Rev. Stephanie Anna Hixon (phone)
July 10, 2018	Rev. Nancy Grissom Self (phone)

Appendix B

BEING FIRST

First Woman Elected Bishop	Marjorie Swank Matthews
First Woman Elected to the Episcopacy from Their Annual (Home) Conference	Matthews, Kelly, Craig, Morrison, Christopher, Sherer, Swenson, Kammerer, Hassinger, Huie, Shamana, Lee, Ward, Kiesey, Middleton, Taylor, Carcaño, Wenner, Nhanala, Ball, Wallace-Padgett, Lewis, Malone, Easterling, Oliveto
First Woman to Serve as Bishop in Conference to Which They Were Assigned	Matthews, Kelly, Craig (twice), Morrison (twice), Christopher (twice), Sherer (twice), Swenson (twice), Kammerer (twice), Hassinger, Huie (twice), Fisher, Ward (twice), Kiesey, Middleton (twice), Taylor (twice), Dyck, Carcaño, Wenner, Stanovsky, Nhanala, Steiner Ball, Wallace-Padgett, Haupert-Johnson, Moore-KoiKoi, Malone, Easterling, Haller
First Woman to Hold Office in the Council of Bishops	Rader (secretary and ecumenical officer), Christopher (president)

First Woman to Deliver Episcopal Address to General Conference	Craig
First Woman to Preside at General Conference	Matthews
First Woman to Preach at General Conference	Matthews
First Woman Elected to Episcopacy in	
Europe	Wenner
Africa	Nhanala
Philippines	To Be Determined
USA	Matthews
First African American Woman Bishop	Kelly
First Hispanic Woman Bishop	Carcaño
First Native American Woman Bishop	To Be Determined
First Woman Bishop of Asian Descent	To Be Determined
First Woman Bishop to Speak at World Methodist Conference	Matthews
First Woman Bishop to Speak at World Council of Churches	Matthews
First Woman Bishop to Hold Office in World Council of Churches	Swenson

Appendix C

WOMEN BISHOPS IN THE UNITED METHODIST CHURCH: 1980–2016

Year Elected	Bishop	Jurisdiction Elected In	Conference Elected From	Area(s) Served [#Years]
1980	Marjorie Swank Matthews	NCJ	W Michigan	Wisconsin [4]
1984	Leontine T. C. Kelly	WJ	Virginia	Cal-Nev [4]
	Judith Craig	NCJ	E Ohio	Michigan [8], West Ohio [8]
1988	Susan Murch Morrison	NEJ	Baltimore-Washington	Philadelphia [8], Albany [8]
	Sharon Brown Christopher	NCJ	Wisconsin	Minnesota [8], IL Great Rivers [8]
1992	Ann Brookshire Sherer	SCJ	Texas	Missouri [12], Nebraska [8]
	Sharon Zimmerman Rader	NCJ	W Michigan	Wisconsin [12]
	Mary Ann Swenson	WJ	Pacific Northwest	Rocky Mtn [8], Cal-Pac [12]

1996	Charlene Payne Kammerer	SEJ	Florida	W NC [8], Virginia [8]
	Susan Wolfe Hassinger	NEJ	E Pennsylvania	Boston [8]
	Janice Riggle Huie	SCJ	SW Texas	Arkansas [8], Texas [12]
2000	Beverly J. Shamana	WJ	Cal-Pac	Cal-Nev [8]
	Violet L. Fisher	NEJ	E Pennsylvania	W NY [8]
	Linda Lee	NCJ	Detroit	Michigan [4], Wisconsin [8]
2004	Hope Morgan Ward	SEJ	North Carolina	Mississippi [8], NC [current]
	Deborah L. Kiesey	NCJ	Iowa	Dakotas [8], Michigan [4]
	Jane Allen Middleton	NEJ	New York	Harrisburg [8], New York [1.5]
	Mary Virginia Taylor	SEJ	Holston	Columbia (SC) [8], Holston [current]
	Sally Dyck	NCJ	E Ohio	Minnesota [8], N Illinois [current]
	Minerva G. Carcaño	WJ	Oregon-Idaho	Phoenix [8], Cal-Pac [4], Cal-Nev [current]
2005	Rosemarie J. Wenner	CC	Germany	Germany [12]
2008	Peggy A. Johnson	NEJ	Baltimore-Washington	Philadelphia [current]
	Elaine J. W. Stanovsky	WJ	Pacific Northwest	Mtn Sky [8], Greater Northwest [current]
	Joaquina Filipe Nhanala	CC	Mozambique	Mozambique [current]
2012	Sandra Lynn Steiner Ball	NEJ	Peninsula-Delaware	W Virginia [current]
	Debra Wallace-Padgett	SEJ	Kentucky	N Alabama [current]

	Cynthia Fierro Harvey	SCJ	SW Texas	Louisiana [current]
2016	Sharma Lewis	SEJ	N Georgia	Virginia [current]
	Sue Haupert-Johnson	SEJ	Florida	N Georgia [current]
	Cynthia Moore-KoiKoi	NEJ	Baltimore-Washington	W Pennsylvania [current]
	Tracy Smith Malone	NCJ	N Illinois	E Ohio [current]
	LaTrelle Easterling	NEJ	New England	Baltimore-WA [current]
	Laurie Haller	NCJ	W Michigan	Iowa [current]
	Karen Oliveto	WJ	Cal-Nevada	Mtn Sky [current]